CONFLICT IN *Mark*

Fortress Press Books
by
Jack Dean Kingsbury

Matthew: Structure, Christology, Kingdom (1975)

Jesus Christ in Matthew, Mark, and Luke
(Proclamation Commentary, 1981)

Matthew (Proclamation Commentary, 1986)
(Second Edition, revised and enlarged)

Matthew as Story
(Second edition, revised and enlarged, 1986)

Conflict in Luke:
Jesus, Authorities, Disciples (1991)

JACK DEAN KINGSBURY

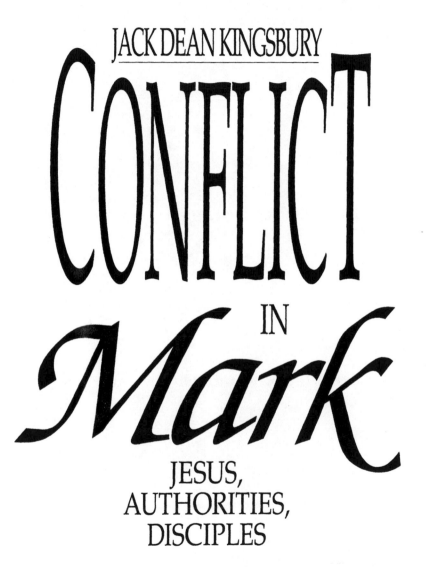

CONFLICT

IN

Mark

JESUS,
AUTHORITIES,
DISCIPLES

FORTRESS PRESS/Minneapolis

To
John F. Byerly, Jr.

Scripture quotations, unless otherwise noted or translated by the author directly from the Hebrew or Greek, are from the Revised Standard Version of the Bible, copyright 1946, 1952, © 1971, 1973 by the Division of Christian Education of the National Council of Churches of Christ in the U.S.A., and are used by permission.

Library of Congress Cataloging-in-Publication Data

Kingsbury, Jack Dean.
   Conflict in Mark : Jesus, authorities, disciples / Jack Dean Kingsbury.
       p.   cm.
   Bibliography: p.
   Includes index.
   ISBN 0–8006–2336–3
   1. Bible. N.T. Mark—Criticism, interpretation, etc.
   2. Jesus Christ—History of doctrines—Early church,
   ca. 30–600. 3. Authority—Biblical teaching. 4. Christian life—
   Biblical teaching. I. Title.
   BS2585.2.K57   1989
   226'.306—dc19   89–1229
                                                                    CIP

Printed in the United States of America   1–2336

4   5   6   7   8   9   10

Contents

Preface

This book is for pastors and students, for use in the study and in the classroom. Each summer, Union Theological Seminary, Virginia, sponsors the Conference on Interpreting the Faith. The invitation to address the Conference on the Gospel according to Mark provided the impetus to write this book.

In the gospel story he narrates, Mark tells, of course, of Jesus. Intertwined with the story of Jesus, however, are two other story lines: that of the religious authorities and that of the disciples. The goal of this book is to trace and interpret all three story lines (chaps. 2–4). To facilitate the reading of each line, chapter 1 deals with important introductory matters.

The development of each story line is determined by themes peculiar to it. In telling of Jesus, for example, Mark interrelates identity with destiny. Not until Jesus' destiny of death on the cross has been narrated does any human other than Jesus himself perceive the mystery of his identity as the Son of God, the kingly figure in whom God is decisively at work to save. By tracing the contours not only of Jesus' ministry but also of the gradual unveiling of his identity, one can highlight this interrelatedness of identity and destiny.

Characteristic of the story of the religious authorities is that they act as ones "without authority." To be without authority is to be without divine authority, to view reality in human, this-worldly terms and not as God would have one view it. Accordingly, the religious authorities are blind to the fact that in Jesus, God in his end-time rule has drawn near to humankind. They oppose Jesus from the outset and very early in the story conspire to bring about his death. They perceive Jesus to be the agent of Satan, a mortal threat to law, tradition, and temple; to themselves as Israel's leaders; and to Israel itself.

The story of the disciples is that of followers of Jesus who are at once loyal to him yet uncomprehending. Called by Jesus to follow him, the disciples leave behind their former way of life and join themselves to him in giving him their total allegiance. Despite their promising beginning, their empowerment by Jesus, and their being given the secret of the kingdom of God, the disciples nonetheless evince a human, this-worldly perspective in most of what they say and do. The upshot is that in situations calling for insight, faith, confession, or action, they tend to fail miserably in one respect or another. Worst of all, they also show as the story progresses that they have no grasp of the true meaning of discipleship. The result is that during Jesus' passion they all break the bond of allegiance and desert him. Mark does not explicitly tell the reader what becomes of the disciples. Instead, he leaves it to the reader to project their fate. What this projection is to be we discuss in chapter 4.

One of the great joys of completing a book is the opportunity it affords to thank those who have so graciously assisted one along the way. In particular, I should like to express my gratitude to Harold W. Rast and John A. Hollar of Fortress Press, for commissioning the manuscript and steering it through to publication; to W. Guy Delaney, until returning to the pastorate Director of Continuing Education at Union Theological Seminary, for the invitation to address the Conference on Interpreting the Faith; to Mark Allan Powell of Trinity Lutheran Seminary, for perusing the final manuscript to gauge its readability; to David A. Handy, my graduate assistant, for preparing the index; and to my wife, Barbara, without whose keen wit and kind ways any project would seem arduous.

J.D.K.

Union Theological Seminary in Virginia
Pentecost Season, 1988

1 | Introduction

*M*ark's story of Jesus is one of swift action and high drama. Only twice, in chapters 4 and 13, does Jesus pause to deliver extended discourses. Following a brief sketch of the ministry of John the Baptist, Mark plunges at once into his narration of Jesus' own ministry, which reaches its culmination in Jesus' death and resurrection. To heighten our appreciation of Mark's story, we begin by exploring several of its features.

The World of the Story

One of the most important features of Mark's story is the world it conjures up. In the act of reading or hearing Mark's story, one temporarily abandons one's twentieth-century surroundings, imaginatively enters the story's first-century world, and dwells in it for a time. One impulse that gave rise to this story is the conviction that human history is the site of a cosmic struggle between God and Satan. God is at work in Jesus to defeat Satan and his minions and to summon Israel (and the nations) to repent, to believe in the gospel, and to live in the sphere of his end-time rule. This conviction explains why no impenetrable barriers exist in Mark's world between the realms of the supernatural and the ordinary. God's voice sounds from heaven; the Spirit descends in the form of a

1

dove; Satan puts Jesus to the test and strives to work his will in the world; angels minister to Jesus; demons shout aloud when confronted by Jesus; John and especially Jesus predict future events; and Jesus, who speaks and acts on divine authority, becomes embroiled in conflict with Satan, demons, and all those who "think the things not of God, but of humans." The unusual and the extraordinary are not alien to the world of Mark's story but belong to the very stuff of this world.

Despite the obvious prominence of the supernatural, the focus of attention within the world of Mark's story is on the realm of human reality. The world of Mark's story is quite unlike the world of much contemporary apocalyptic literature.[1] Here the focus is often on otherworldly journeys to heaven, Sheol, or the ends of the earth, or on heavenly visions in which the course of history is reviewed and revealed. By contrast, the boundaries circumscribing Mark's world are more narrowly drawn and are both spatial and temporal in nature.

Spatially, although the world of Mark's story may be said to encompass heaven, earth, and Gehenna (hell), heaven and Gehenna are never described but only referred to in passing. Moreover, although the barriers separating heaven and earth are such that earth is open to heaven, the distinction between these two realms remains intact. Heaven is the abode of God, his angels, the exalted Jesus, and the ultimate home of the elect. Here God's will is done and his rule encounters no opposition. In Jesus of Nazareth, God draws near in his rule to humankind. Humans are summoned by Jesus to repent and believe the gospel, become his followers, and enter even now into the sphere of God's rule. At the end of the age, however, the exalted Jesus shall return to earth and usher in the rule of God in power. At that time, opposition to God's rule will end also on earth, and God through Jesus will reign supreme.

In speaking of the nearness of God's rule, we have already touched on the temporal dimensions of the world of Mark's story. All of time is divided into two great segments: the present age and the age to come. Since little is said of the latter, attention is centered on the former. Beginning with creation, the present age extends to the final judgment at the end of human history. It too is made up of two segments or, more exactly, two epochs. The dividing line separating these epochs is the appearance of John the Baptist and Jesus. The epoch preceding John and Jesus is the time of prophecy; the epoch they inaugurate is the time of fulfillment. More particularly, the time of fulfillment is the time of the gospel. It encompasses the ministries to Israel of John, Jesus, and the pre-Easter disciples, and the ministry to the nations of the post-Easter disciples. Not until the return of the exalted Jesus to earth and the establishment of God's rule in power will the time of the gospel have run its course and the present age have given way to the age to come.

Settings

A second notable feature of the story that Mark tells is the larger setting of the story and the many settings within the story. A "setting" is the place, time, or social circumstances in which any character acts.[2] Within a story, settings[3] may be minimal or highly charged with meaning. Minimal settings simply make action possible. Mark, for example, frequently uses the single word "and" or the expression "and immediately" as a temporal marker to link one scene or episode with another and thereby indicate the passage of time.[4] An example of a temporal setting highly charged with meaning is Jesus' announcement in Galilee of the beginning of a new epoch in history, the time of the gospel: Jesus proclaims, "The time is fulfilled and the kingdom of God has drawn near; repent and believe in the gospel!" (1:14-15).

As to locale, the larger setting of Mark's story is, above all, the land of the Jews.[5] In Mark as in Matthew and Luke as well, Jesus' ministry is broadly depicted as a journey: first, within and around Galilee; and then on the way to, and in and about, Jerusalem. Baptized in the River Jordan and put

to the test in the desert, Jesus discharges his ministry beside
the Sea of Galilee, in Capernaum, in synagogues and houses,
in boats and atop mountains, in deserted places and out on
the sea, in gentile territories, in Bethsaida, in the regions of
Judea and across the Jordan, in Jericho, in and around Jerusalem (especially Bethany and the Mount of Olives), and
in the temple.

Within their larger setting, many of the places just cited
are of no little significance in their own right. For example,
the "desert" is at once the place to which John summons Israel
to repentance and end-time renewal and in which Satan is at
home and puts Jesus to the test.[6] "Galilee" is the region where
Jesus discharges his public ministry to Israel: He preaches,
calls disciples, teaches, heals, and exorcises demons.[7] After
his resurrection, Jesus will also return to Galilee.[8] By contrast,
"Jerusalem" is a place of danger and condemnation to death.[9]
Jesus' enemies are at home here, and from here scribes and
Pharisees come to Galilee to attack him and his disciples.[10]
And the "temple,"[11] the house of God's presence and the seat
of the religious authorities' power, is a place of intense conflict: Prior to his passion, Jesus' last great confrontation with
the religious authorities occurs here. As is plain, therefore,
settings make no small contribution to both the tenor and the
tone of Mark's story.

Characters

The persons or groups of persons who inhabit the world
of Mark's story constitute yet another significant feature of
this story. Four major characters[12] stand out, as do two groups
of minor characters: Jesus, the religious authorities, the disciples, the crowd, and those groups of minor characters who
either exhibit faith or somehow exemplify what it means to
serve.

Jesus

Jesus is the protagonist of Mark's story. Of the major characters, he is the one who always views reality—what is good

or bad, right or wrong, true or false—the way God does. Because Mark establishes God's understanding of reality as normative within his story, Jesus is supremely the one who "thinks the things of God."[13] What Jesus approves or disapproves of, be it persons or events, the reader is invited to approve or disapprove of. Fundamentally, Jesus is the character who determines the plot, or flow of events, in Mark's story.

In the parable of the wicked husbandmen (12:1-12), Mark presents Jesus as disclosing in capsule form how he understands himself, his relationship to God, and his place in the history of salvation. Jesus knows God to be his Father,[14] himself to be the Son of God in whom God in his end-time rule draws near to humankind,[15] and his mission to be of decisive significance for both Israel and the gentiles.[16] An essential part of Jesus' mission is to establish the end-time people of God.[17]

Although Jesus knows himself to be the Son of God sent by God, his identity as such is by no means apparent to all other characters in Mark's story. To appreciate this, one may observe how other characters construe Jesus' identity. Though not a character, Mark as narrator nonetheless affirms at the start that Jesus is Israel's Messiah, the Son of God (1:1). For his part, John the Baptist thinks of Jesus as the mightier One, God's agent of salvation (1:7-8). In the baptismal pericope and also at the transfiguration, God announces that Jesus is his beloved Son (1:11; 9:7). Because the temptation is tied to the baptism, Mark invites the reader to infer that Satan too recognizes that Jesus is God's Son and puts him to the test as such (1:12-13). To their dread, demons, or unclean spirits, likewise recognize that Jesus is God's Son.[18] By contrast, the religious authorities look upon Jesus as the agent of Satan, or Beelzebul,[19] the prince of demons (3:22, 30). In Nazareth, Jesus' family, relatives, and acquaintances cannot believe that he is anyone other than the carpenter, the son of Mary (6:3). Hearing reports of Jesus, Herod Antipas chooses to regard Jesus as John the Baptist, whom he has beheaded, come back to life (6:14-16). Similarly, the Jewish crowd too regards Jesus as a prophet: John the Baptist raised from the dead, Elijah, or some other prophet (6:14-16; 8:28). Speaking on behalf of the disciples, Peter confesses Jesus to be the Messiah, in response to which Jesus commands him to silence (8:29-30). Appealing for mercy and healing, blind Bartimaeus calls upon Jesus as the Son of David (10:47-48). As Jesus is about to enter Jerusalem, the throng surrounding him hails him as the One coming in the name of the Lord who is the bearer of the coming kingdom of their father David (11:9-10). Pilate and the mocking soldiers, in turn, refer to Jesus as the King of the Jews, which to their way of thinking makes him out to be an insurrectionist.[20] Finally, at the foot of the cross the Roman centurion, observing the manner in which Jesus dies, acclaims him to have been the Son of God (15:39).

What these diverse views of Jesus' identity reveal is the sharp cleavage one finds in Mark's story between the way supernatural beings and Mark as narrator perceive Jesus and the way humans perceive him. On the one hand, Mark as narrator and supernatural beings such as God, Satan, and demons know exactly who Jesus is: the Son of God. On the other hand, humans experience Jesus not only as an extraordinary figure but also as an immensely controversial one. They regard him in numerous, conflicting ways that run the gamut from abject repudiation as the agent of Satan to acclamation as the Son of God. In point of fact, the centurion at the cross is the only human other than Jesus himself to recognize Jesus to be the Son of God and thus to express an understanding of him that tallies with God's understanding. This shows, therefore, that, for humans, Jesus' identity remains surrounded by an aura of mystery until the end of Mark's story. Moreover, it also suggests that humans cannot perceive aright who Jesus is until they view his entire life and ministry from the perspective of the cross. To view Jesus from any other perspective is in some sense inadequate or wholly false.

In the course of Mark's story, Jesus exhibits, by what he says and does or what is narrated of him, a multiplicity of character traits. Still, all of Jesus' character traits ultimately spring from one root trait, to wit: that Jesus is "uniquely related" to God his Father (1:11; 9:7; 12:6).[21] By virtue of this unique relationship, Jesus is who he is, the Son of God, and his mission accomplishes salvation for all humankind, Jew and gentile alike (14:24).

Uniquely related to God, Jesus evinces such traits as the following: (*a*) Relative to his mission, Jesus is "authoritative" (1:10).[22] Empowered by God's Spirit, Jesus withstands the testing of Satan, preaches the gospel of God's end-time rule, calls disciples, teaches God's will, heals the sick, exorcises demons, bests his opponents in debate, and goes the way of the cross. In Jesus, God is decisively at work to accomplish universal salvation. (*b*) Toward God, Jesus is "whole," for he loves God with heart, soul, mind, and strength (12:29-30). Jesus loves God with all his heart, for he is perfectly obedient to God (1:12-13). Jesus loves God with all his soul, for in doing God's will he does not withhold even the giving of his life (14:36; 15:37). And Jesus loves God with all his mind and strength, for he lays no claim for himself to either the prerogatives of worldly power or the security of home, family, and possessions.[23] (*c*) Toward himself, Jesus possesses "integrity."[24] As one observes Jesus throughout Mark's story, one discovers that no discrepancy exists between what he says and what he does. On the contrary, Jesus' teaching is embodied in his behavior, and his behavior attests to the truth of his teaching.[25] (*d*) Toward the disciples, Jesus is "enabling" and "faithful"; yet they also "vex" him. In calling the disciples, Jesus empowers them to leave behind their former way of life and to follow him and be with him.[26] Still, because of their persistent incomprehension, they also annoy and exasperate him.[27] Nevertheless, at the same time as he predicts that they will betray, forsake, and deny him, he also graciously promises them that he will reconcile them to himself.[28] (*e*) Toward the Jewish crowd and minor characters of faith, Jesus is "compassionate." Jesus has profound pity on the crowd, for he recognizes that they are leaderless, like sheep without a shepherd (6:34). Similarly, he heals afflicted individuals when they, or others on their behalf, appeal to him in trust that he can restore them.[29] (*f*) Toward the religious authorities, Jesus is "confrontational." Jesus clashes continually with the authorities, for they refuse the summons of both John and himself to repent and they see in him the agent of Satan instead of the agent of God.[30] *(g)* Toward his death, Jesus is "self-giving." The essence of "wholeness" is love of God and love of neighbor. Love of neighbor is not lording it over others but serving them (10:42-45). Jesus serves all others (10:45), for he "pours out" his blood to establish a new covenant and atone for the sins of "many," Jews and gentiles alike (14:24; 15:38).

Disciples

If Jesus is the protagonist of Mark's story who always "thinks the things of God," the disciples constitute a character who possesses conflicting traits. The initial impression the reader gets of the disciples is that they too "think the things of God." After all, they are not the opponents of Jesus but his followers. Still, as Mark's story progresses, the disciples seem ever more prone to "think the things of humans." The result is that increasingly the reader is invited to look upon them with disapproval. Except perhaps for Judas, the disciples do not greatly influence the plot, or course of events, in Mark's story. Nonetheless, the conflict between them and Jesus is sharp and profound, for at issue is the meaning of discipleship. How this conflict is ultimately resolved is not explicitly narrated by Mark. Instead, Mark leaves it to the reader to use his or her imagination to project its outcome. The exact contours of this outcome will be discussed in chapter 4.

In citing the names of the twelve (3:16-20), Mark shows that when he speaks of the disciples he generally has the twelve in view. Even before Jesus actually creates the circle of the twelve, Mark employs the term "disciples" in anticipation of its formation, that is, he presupposes its existence.[31] To be sure, Mark at points highlights the group of four (Peter, James, John, and Andrew; 13:3), or the two sets of brothers (Simon and Andrew; James and John),[32] or the group of three (Peter, James, and John)[33] or simply Peter,[34] John (9:38), or Judas.[35] This notwithstanding, Mark makes no fundamental distinction between these individuals or smaller groups and the twelve. On the contrary, the special roles Peter and Judas play have to do with the fact that Judas betrays Jesus[36] and Peter is both the spokesman of the disciples and, in his behavior, typical of them.[37] Though a group, the disciples plainly stand out as a single character.

Mark makes known the character traits of the disciples primarily through their interaction with Jesus and only secondarily through their interaction with other characters. If the many traits Jesus exhibits spring from one root trait, the many traits the disciples exhibit spring from two conflicting traits: The disciples are at once "loyal"[38] and "uncomprehending." On the one hand, the disciples are "loyal": Jesus summons them to follow him and they immediately leave behind their former way of life and give him their total allegiance.[39] On the other hand, the disciples are "uncomprehending": Understanding fully neither the identity nor the destiny of Jesus and not at all the essential meaning of discipleship, they forsake Jesus during his passion.

Not until the middle of his story (1:14—8:26), after Jesus has begun his ministry, does Mark introduce the reader to the first disciples (1:16-20). Initially, Mark casts the disciples in a highly favorable light: He depicts them as being "loyal" and, in connection with this, as also being "committed," "authoritative," "observant," "obedient," "enlightened," "supportive," and "vulnerable." At heart "loyal," the disciples are "committed" and "authoritative," for Jesus imparts to them authority and they enthusiastically embrace a ministry to Israel patterned after his own: They preach, teach, heal, and exorcise demons.[40] The disciples are "observant," for they remain "with Jesus," bearing witness to what he says and does (3:14). The disciples are "obedient," for Jesus commands and they comply.[41] The disciples are "enlightened," for God discloses to them the mystery of his kingdom (4:11) and Jesus explains to them the meaning of his parables (4:34). The disciples are "supportive," for although Jesus must defend them in controversy, they nonetheless stand at his side.[42] And the disciples are "vulnerable," for they risk attack by the religious authorities precisely because they follow Jesus.[13]

Interlaced with these favorable traits are also conflicting, negative traits. As we noted, however, Mark traces the many character flaws of the disciples to one fundamental flaw: They are "uncomprehending" in either mind or heart or both. The upshot is that the disciples likewise reveal themselves, in the middle of Mark's story, to be "cowardly," "bereft of faith," "fearful," "distraught," groundlessly "astonished," and "hard of heart."

For example, although enlightened by God, who gives them the mystery of his kingdom, the disciples do not, as Jesus expects, understand his parables (4:13; 7:17-18). Moreover, in three boat scenes and two feeding miracles they further evince a striking lack of understanding. In the first boat scene, the disciples show that they have not perceived who Jesus is (4:41): Far from resting secure in his sustaining presence when threatened by a storm, they prove themselves to be "cowardly," "bereft of faith," and "fearful" (4:40-41). In the two feeding miracles, the disciples, though endowed by Jesus with authority, nonetheless become "distraught" and treat as fantasy Jesus' challenge that they feed the five thousand (6:35-37) and the four thousand (8:2-4). In the second boat scene, the disciples, having now witnessed Jesus himself feed the five thousand, still demonstrate their inability to comprehend either the dimensions of his divine authority or that they can rest secure in his sustaining presence: Encountering a heavy wind and seeing Jesus walk on water, they think him to be a ghost and, becoming "fearful," they cry aloud in terror (6:48-50); and after Jesus has caused the wind to abate, they are, for sheer lack of comprehension, "astonished" at his feat (6:51-52). And in the second and third boat scenes, the disciples, having seen Jesus feed the five thousand prior to the one scene and both the five thousand and the four thousand prior to the other, yet fail so completely to grasp the reality that Jesus is able to meet any need that both Mark as narrator and Jesus castigate them as "hard of heart" (6:52; 8:17-21).

In the end section of Mark's story (8:27—16:8), the disciples become ever more "uncomprehending," until they at last fall away from Jesus. To their credit, they remain "loyal" until Jesus' arrest at Gethsemane (14:50). Accordingly, they still follow him, give him their allegiance, and exhibit positive character traits. To illustrate, the disciples show themselves to be "enlightened" to the extent that Peter, on their behalf, correctly though insufficiently confesses Jesus to be the Messiah (8:29). The disciples are also "observant" in the sense that they continue to be eye- and ear-witnesses to Jesus' words and deeds (e.g., 14:22-25). And the disciples are "obedient," as when Jesus twice sends two of them either to fetch the colt on which he rides into Jerusalem (10:1-7) or to make preparations for the celebration of the Passover meal (14:13-16).

Overall, however, the positive traits of the disciples, which spring from their loyalty to Jesus, pale when compared to the negative traits they display as a result of their gross incomprehension. Throughout the end section of Mark's story, the disciples do not, and will not, understand that the goal of Jesus' ministry is suffering and death (8:31). Unable to understand the nature of Jesus' ministry, the disciples are unable to understand the nature of discipleship, which has its focus in servanthood and not in self-concern (8:34-35). The inability to understand the nature of either Jesus' ministry or discipleship, therefore, is the underlying factor giving rise to the negative traits displayed by the disciples in the end of Mark's story.

On the way to Jerusalem, the disciples attest to their incomprehension by showing themselves to be "unreceptive" to Jesus' teaching, "dense" and "fearful," "ineffectual at healing," "status-conscious," "exclusive," "enamored of wealth," "anxious about the future," and "desirous of power and position." Three times Jesus teaches the disciples through passion predictions that the purpose of his ministry is to suffer and die (8:31; 9:31; 10:33-34). Three times the behavior of the disciples indicates they are "unreceptive" to his teaching.

Following Jesus' first passion prediction, Peter manifests his failure to comprehend Jesus' words by openly rebuking him (8:32-33). Atop the mount of transfiguration, Peter, James, and John prove themselves to be both "dense" and "fearful": They do not grasp the revelation they see and hear but are overcome by fright (9:5-6). Correspondingly, the disciples left below, though they have the authority to cast out demons,[44] do not avail themselves of this authority and hence are "ineffectual" in their attempt to heal the boy with the unclean spirit (9:14-29).

Following Jesus' second passion prediction, Mark bluntly tells the reader that the disciples do not grasp Jesus' teaching (9:32), and the disciples confirm this by demonstrating that they are "status-conscious," "exclusive," "enamored of wealth," and "anxious about the future." The disciples are "status-conscious," for they quarrel over who among them is greatest (9:34) and attempt to turn away those bringing children to Jesus for blessing (9:13-14). They are "exclusive," for they would forbid one who is not a member of their circle from exorcising demons in Jesus' name (9:38-40). They are "enamored of wealth," for they espouse the conventional wisdom that sees in wealth a sign of God's special favor (10:23-27). And they are "anxious about the future," for Peter demands to know of Jesus what they, who have left all to follow him, can anticipate the future will hold for them (10:28-31).

Following Jesus' third passion prediction, the disciples once again reveal that his words have fallen on uncomprehending ears. No sooner has Jesus uttered his prediction than James and John, "desirous of power and position," approach him requesting for themselves the places of greatest honor in his glory (10:35-40). The ten take umbrage at this, not because their motives are purer, but because they desire these places for themselves (10:41).

Once Jesus has arrived in Jerusalem and entered on his passion, the disciples' incomprehension renders them unfit to cope with events and they forsake Jesus. Indicative of their incomprehension is the fact that they are "imperceptive," "self-deluded," and "disloyal"; in addition, Judas becomes both "deceitful" and "treacherous" and Peter "apostate."

In the house of Simon the leper, the disciples are seemingly among those indignantly scolding the woman who has poured expensive nard ointment on the head of Jesus (14:3-9). Ironically, their indignation at alleged waste is in fact a sign that they are "imperceptive" to the true meaning of her act: She has anointed Jesus' body for burial (14:8). At the last supper, Judas discloses that he is at heart "deceitful." Along with the other disciples, he asks Jesus whether he will be the one to betray him in such manner as to anticipate that Jesus' answer will be, "No" (14:19). Judas' deceit is that he has already visited the religious authorities and made his pact with them to betray Jesus (14:10-11). At the Mount of Olives and at Gethsemane, the disciples stand out as hopelessly "self-deluded." Arriving with Jesus at the Mount of Olives, Peter, joined by the others, insists with great confidence that he will die with Jesus rather than deny him (14:31). At Gethsemane, however, Peter, James, and John put the lie to the confidence they just expressed: Far from suffering death with Jesus, they cannot summon the strength even to watch with him for an hour but instead fall asleep (14:37, 40-41). Finally, the arrest of Jesus and the events surrounding his trial become the place in Mark's story where the reader at last witnesses the ultimate result of the disciples' incomprehension: (*a*) Judas, who has already been "deceitful," now becomes "treacherous" as well and betrays Jesus (14:43-46). (*b*) All the disciples become "disloyal" by breaking the bond of their allegiance to Jesus and fleeing (14:50). And (*c*) Peter, by denying Jesus, becomes "apostate" (14:54, 66-72).

In sum, the multiplicity of character traits the disciples exhibit in Mark's story stems from two fundamentally conflicting traits: The disciples are at once "loyal" and "uncomprehending." Of these two traits, the incomprehension of the disciples seems finally to dominate and to snuff out their loyalty to Jesus. This notwithstanding, Mark's final word on the disciples is one not of disloyalty but of promise. Even while predicting that the disciples will fall away from him, Jesus makes them a pledge: After he has been raised, he will go before them into Galilee where, the young man in white at the tomb adds, they will see him (14:28; 16:7). The reason the reader is ultimately to think of the disciples as reconciled followers of Jesus and not as rank apostates has to do with the way he or she is invited to view Jesus' promise to the disciples as determining their relationship to him following the resurrection.

Religious Authorities

The antagonists of Jesus in Mark's story are the religious authorities, whether scribes, Pharisees, Herodians,[15] Sadducees, chief priests, or elders.[16] They are the rulers in Israel, entrusted by God with the care of Israel. They see in Jesus a mortal threat to both themselves and the people. Except perhaps for the "friendly scribe," the authorities form a united front against Jesus and thus constitute a single character. Next to Jesus, they are the ones who influence most the plot of Mark's story.

Mark develops his characterization of the religious authorities through their interaction with Jesus and, to a minor extent, through their interaction with the disciples and the Jewish crowd. Mark himself also provides the reader with commentary about them which is highly unflattering. Just as the many character traits Jesus exhibits all stem from one root trait (being "uniquely related" to God), so the many character traits the authorities exhibit all stem from one root trait, to wit: They are "without authority" (1:22). To be without authority is to be without divine authority and therefore to "think the things of humans" instead of "the things of God" (8:33). It is, in fact, to be on the side of Satan (8:33). As a result, the character traits Mark ascribes to the religious authorities (save, again, for the "friendly scribe") are uniformly negative. In approaching Mark's portrait of the authorities, the reader can anticipate that it will be harsh and polemical and that he or she will consistently be invited to distance himself or herself from them.

In Mark's story, the religious authorities are Israel's "leaders."[47] Like the disciples, they too make their debut in the middle of the story (1:14—8:26), after Jesus has begun his ministry. The first thing Mark tells the reader of them, before they themselves have even had opportunity to speak or act, is that they are, in the persons of the scribes, "without authority" (1:22). As leaders without authority, the authorities, as we noted, view reality from a human standpoint instead of from God's standpoint. The many character traits they evince well attest to this.

As leaders who think the things of humans, the religious authorities are "hypocritical" in their practice of religion. In Mark's story world, hypocrisy exists where there is a discrepancy between appearance and underlying truth.[18] When judged by this standard, the authorities are hypocritical in their religious practice in relation to both God and the people. The Pharisees and the scribes are hypocritical toward God, for while they ostensibly teach God's word and will, in reality they teach the "commandments of men" (7:6-7). And the scribes are hypocritical toward the people, for their religiosity masks a desire that great deference and honor be paid them (12:38-40). Indeed, one of the many ironies typifying the religious authorities is that they perceive themselves to be "righteous" (2:17). In their own eyes, they are the ones who know and do God's will.

Thinking as they do the things of humans, the religious authorities are also "in error," which is to say that they are false teachers.[49] The true teacher in Mark's story world is, of course, Jesus. One way Mark stresses this is by having the "friendly scribe," who is himself one of the authorities, pay tribute to Jesus' superior knowledge of the law (12:28, 32-33). By the same token, the best index of the falseness of the authorities' teaching is the way they deal with the law and, more broadly, all scripture.

Although the religious authorities esteem themselves to be expert in matters of scripture and therefore of law and religion, Jesus shows that they are "unable to read" scripture so as to discern its meaning.[50] The authorities, he charges, do not "know" scripture (12:24). Scripture predicts that Elijah will come and restore all things, but the authorities are blind

to the fact that Elijah has already come in the person of John
the Baptist and they have repudiated him (9:11-13; 11:31).
Scripture also says that Jesus himself must suffer and be rejected, but the insight that the way the authorities have treated
John presages the way they will treat him has eluded them
(9:12-13). And if scripture tells the authorities that the Messiah is the Son of David, the fact that it likewise tells them
that the Messiah is more than the Son of David (and is indeed
the Son of God) escapes them (12:35-37).[51]

Lacking true knowledge, the religious authorities furthermore "misinterpret" scripture to make it serve their purposes.
Although Mosaic law commands that parents be honored, the
Pharisees and the scribes allow children to nullify this command by denying their parents the support they are otherwise
obligated to give them: Children set aside for their own use
the support they owe their parents by declaring it to be a gift
dedicated to God (7:10-13). Although Mosaic law itself reveals
that God's intention at creation was that divorce not be per-
mitted, the Pharisees wrongly appeal to the "concession" Moses made to the hardness of the human heart in order to
justify divorce (10:2-9). And although the book of Moses attests to the resurrection of the dead, the Sadducees stoutly
deny there is any such thing (12:18-27).

As if to compound their misuse of scripture, the religious
authorities even "disobey" it outright. In their supervision of
the temple, the chief priests, instead of honoring God's command that his house be a place of prayer for all the nations,
have in reality turned the temple into their own sacrilegious
preserve (11:17).

Finally, the extreme irony of the way the religious authorities relate to scripture is that they do not see that it actually
"prophesies against them." Thus, the word Isaiah uttered
condemns the Pharisees and the scribes: While claiming to
teach God's word, they promulgate instead their own doctrines as embodied in the tradition of the elders (7:6-13). And
the word the psalmist spoke is a prediction the chief priests,
scribes, and elders are tragically rushing headlong to fulfill:
In telling of "the builders" who "reject the very stone" God

will place at the head of the corner, the psalmist foretold the death of Jesus, God's Son, at their hands and Jesus' vindication by God in the resurrection (12:10-11).

In addition to being "hypocritical" and "in error," the religious authorities, as leaders thinking the things of humans, are furthermore "hard of heart" (3:5). To be hard of heart means to be "loveless" and "legalistic." When Jesus does good on the sabbath and heals the man with the withered hand, the Pharisees, with the Herodians, do not rejoice but instead find in this an infraction of the sabbath law; indeed, they turn the sabbath into the day they themselves do evil and conspire how to destroy Jesus (3:1-6). In point of fact, the "friendly scribe" himself puts his finger on the fundamental difference separating Jesus and the religious authorities in terms of what it is to do the will of God: Whereas the essential matter for Jesus is loving God and neighbor, for the authorities it is strict adherence to law and tradition as they define this.[52]

As leaders who are without authority and think the things of humans, the religious authorities interact with Jesus, the disciples, and the crowd. From the outset, the authorities are "implacably opposed" to Jesus (2:1—3:6). They do not receive him as the Messiah Son of God in whom God in his end-time rule has graciously drawn near and who therefore calls Israel to repentance and belief in the gospel. On the contrary, they regard him as the agent of Satan[53] who, because of his alleged assault on law,[54] tradition,[55] and temple,[56] threaten their overthrow as Israel's leaders[57] and Israel's very ruin.

In their encounters with Jesus throughout Mark's story, the authorities exhibit numerous traits that spring from their implacable opposition to him. (*a*) Like Satan himself, the authorities are "tempting" in that they repeatedly put Jesus to the test. The Pharisees call upon Jesus to prove that he acts on the authority of God and not Satan by specifying a sign God is to perform in their sight (8:11-13). Apparently aware of Jesus' categorical stand against divorce, the Pharisees also challenge Jesus to prove that he does not teach counter to Moses' permission of divorce (10:2-9). And the Pharisees and the Herodians attempt to entice Jesus to say whether the law sanctions paying the poll tax to Caesar in the confidence he can answer neither "Yes" nor "No" without incriminating himself: Should he say, "Yes," he risks offending Jews by seemingly placing Caesar above God and recognizing as legitimate a tax symbolizing subjugation to Rome. Should he say, "No," he risks making himself out to be a revolutionary in the eyes of Romans (12:13-17). (*b*) The authorities are "hypocritical" in their exchanges with Jesus. Although the Pharisees and the scribes claim, in insisting on observance of the tradition of the elders, that they uphold God's will, in truth they nullify God's word and foster their own doctrines (7:5-13). And the Pharisees and the Herodians, by inviting Jesus to declare whether or not the law sanctions paying taxes to Caesar, give the appearance of requesting honest information from him, whereas in reality they are looking to catch him in a trap (12:13-17). (*c*) The authorities are "conspiratorial" in their conflict with Jesus. Four times Mark recounts that the Pharisees, the chief priests and the scribes, or the entire Sanhedrin take(s) counsel against Jesus either on how to destroy him[58] or to arrest him[59] or both[60] without stirring up the crowd[61] or on how to proceed in delivering him to Pilate (15:1). (*d*) The authorities are "deceitful," or "cunning," in bringing about the arrest and the death of Jesus (14:1). The chief priests happily accept Judas' offer to betray Jesus and promise him money (14:10-11). The chief priests, scribes, and elders use the crowd who heard Jesus with delight as he daily taught in the temple to arrest him.[62] At Jesus' trial, the chief priests, elders, and scribes, presided over by the high priest, attempt, though unsuccessfully, to get Jesus sentenced to death on the basis of false testimony (14:55-60). And before Pilate, the chief priests falsely accuse Jesus, after he affirms he is the King of the Jews, of sedition against Rome, in the face of which Jesus remains silent (15:2-5). (*e*) The authorities reveal that they are "envious" of Jesus (15:10). As Mark indicates, the hostility the chief priests exhibit toward Jesus at his hearing before Pilate is what convinces Pilate that they act out of envy (15:1-5). (*f*) And the authorities are "blasphemous" toward Jesus. At points during Jesus' ministry or passion, the authorities accuse him of committing blasphemy against God. The irony, however, is that, in attacking Jesus, who is God's Son, they are the ones blaspheming God. When Jesus forgives the paralytic his sins, some of the scribes charge him with blasphemy and thus deny him the authority God gave him to grant forgiveness (2:6-7). Witnessing Jesus' exorcisms, the scribes from Jerusalem commit the unpardonable sin against God's Spirit by declaring that Jesus acts on the authority of Beelzebul, or Satan (3:22, 28-30). At Jesus' trial, the high priest himself becomes blasphemous by turning the truth of Jesus' claim to be the Messiah Son of God into the lie that it is an offense against God's majesty (14:61-64). And as Jesus hangs on the cross, the chief priests with the scribes unwittingly mock God by making mockery of Jesus' affirmation before Pilate that he is in fact the King of the Jews (15:2, 31-32).

If the religious authorities in Mark's story are implacably opposed to Jesus, they are equally "implacably opposed" to the disciples. True, the number of times the authorities confront the disciples is few. Nevertheless, because the disciples follow Jesus, they do as he does. This means that, in the eyes of the authorities, the disciples too threaten the stability of Israel by willfully violating law and tradition.

In their interaction with the disciples, the authorities evince such traits as the following: (*a*) They are "accusatory." When the disciples pluck grain on the sabbath, the Pharisees approach Jesus and charge them with breaking the law by unlawfully reaping on the sabbath (2:23-24). And when the Pharisees and the scribes spot the disciples eating with unwashed (i. e., ritually unclean) hands, they too approach Jesus and demand to know why the disciples transgress the tradition of the elders (7:1-5). (*b*) The authorities are "guileful." When Judas comes and offers to betray Jesus, the chief priests do not turn him away but gladly accept his offer and promise him money (14:10-11). (*c*) And the authorities will, in the future, be "hostile." In his eschatological discourse, Jesus predicts that in the time following the resurrection and leading up to the Parousia, the disciples will, in carrying out their mission to the nations, be delivered up to Jewish councils and beaten in synagogues (13:9-10).

In Mark's story, the religious authorities interact primarily with Jesus and only seldom with either the disciples or the Jewish crowd. Despite such little interaction between authorities and crowd, both character groups make up Israel. In standing opposite Israel, Jesus and the disciples stand opposite these larger groups. In the isolated glimpses Mark provides of the way the authorities relate to the crowd, the traits the authorities display do not, as one might expect, suddenly become positive in nature. To the contrary, they remain harshly negative.

Overall, Mark's characterization of the authorities as they interact with the crowd is that they are "faithless" to their trust. To bring this out, Mark attributes to the authorities such traits as the following: (*a*) The authorities are "remiss" as leaders. On one occasion, Jesus looks out over the crowd and has compassion on them, for they are leaderless, as sheep having no shepherd (6:34). (*b*) The authorities are "fearful" of the crowd. Three times Mark comments that the chief priests and the scribes or the chief priests, scribes, and elders want to move against Jesus but hold back for fear this will cause an uproar among the crowd (11:18; 12:12; 14:1-2). (*c*) The authorities are both "pretentious" and "ostentatious." To be seen by the crowd and to secure for themselves praise and honor, the scribes walk about in special garments, accept deferential greetings in the marketplace, assume the best seats at banquets and in synagogues, and offer long prayers (12:38-40). (*d*) And the authorities are "manipulative." As Pilate endeavors to sway the crowd to request amnesty for Jesus, the chief priests intervene to incite the crowd to call for the release of the murderer Barabbas and for the crucifixion of Jesus (15:9-13).

Stepping back now to look at the whole of Mark's character portrait of the religious authorities, one is struck by the exceedingly dark hues in which it has been painted. This portrait is devoid of pleasant lines calculated to elicit a sympathetic response on the part of the reader toward the authorities. On the contrary, it is unsparing in its severity. In Mark's story, the root trait characterizing the authorities is that they are "without authority." As leaders without authority, the authorities "think the things of humans" and place themselves on the side of Satan. Even the "friendly scribe" serves the purpose of depicting one of Jesus' opponents as acknowledging his superior knowledge of the law and will of God. Throughout the story, the authorities are "implacably opposed" to both Jesus and the disciples. Nor is their relationship to the crowd significantly better, for they display no positive traits but instead prove themselves to be "faithless" to their trust. Mark's portrait is harsh and forbidding indeed.

Crowd

The fourth major character in Mark's story is the Jewish crowd. Together with the religious authorities, it makes up Israel, which stands opposite Jesus. In the peculiar role it plays, however, the crowd contrasts with both the authorities and the disciples. Unlike the authorities, the crowd is not the inveterate enemy of Jesus: Jesus ministers to it and it eagerly searches him out. Unlike the disciples, the crowd never joins itself to Jesus as followers committed to his cause. On the contrary, at Jesus' arrest it unites with the authorities to bring about his death.

The character traits with which Mark endows the crowd come to light through its interaction with Jesus. To contrast particular traits of the crowd with those displayed by the authorities, Mark in at least two episodes juxtaposes a reaction of the crowd to Jesus to a reaction of the authorities. Until Jesus' arrest, Mark generally invites the reader to adopt an attitude of sympathy and approval toward the crowd. Essentially, the crowd exhibits two conflicting traits: It is "well disposed" toward Jesus but also "without faith" in him.

On the one hand, the crowd is "well disposed" toward Jesus. As Jesus traverses Galilee, his fame spreads everywhere.[63] In turn, the crowd searches for Jesus (1:37), comes to him from all directions and from far away,[64] gathers round him,[65] and follows him.[66] Once when he suddenly appears on the scene, the crowd rushes to greet him (9:15). At one point, his popularity becomes so great that he dare not enter a city openly (1:45). Yet, even when he sojourns in deserted places, the crowd flocks to him from everywhere (1:45). On one occasion when he sets sail with the disciples, the crowd sees him and runs on foot to meet him at the landing (6:32-34). Periodically, the press of the crowd becomes so great that it threatens to crush him[67] or prevents him and his disciples from eating.[68] Often Jesus feels the need to escape from the crowd, and he and the disciples do so usually by boat.[69]

Thus far, it seems as though the crowd is well disposed toward Jesus because of his fame and popularity. Not so. The deeper reason, in fact, lies with those activities so typical of his ministry. As Jesus ministers in Israel, he has compassion on the crowd, for it is leaderless, like sheep having no shepherd (6:34). Jesus proclaims the word,[70] and the crowd throngs about him to hear (2:2). He summons persons in the crowd to become his followers,[71] and apparently there are those who respond.[72]

Customarily, Jesus teaches the crowd, as when he is beside the Sea of Galilee or in the temple,[73] and the crowd is amazed at his teaching and gladly listens.[74] He heals the sick and drives out demons,[75] and the crowd is astonished by his powerful acts.[76] Indeed, the crowd brings the sick and demon-possessed to him, and they strive to touch his garments so they may be healed.[77] In two instances, Jesus even feeds crowds of five thousand and of four thousand, in the latter case after all were with him for a period of three days.[78]

In being well disposed toward Jesus, the crowd stands in sharp contrast to its leaders, the religious authorities. Two observations make this plain. On the question of Jesus' identity, the authorities decide early on that Jesus is an agent of Beelzebul, or Satan (3:22, 30). Contrariwise, the crowd concludes that Jesus is a prophet of some stature: John the Baptist raised from the dead, Elijah, or one of the prophets of old.[79] In reality, Jesus is the Messiah, the Son of God. Accordingly, incorrect though the crowd's view may be, it nonetheless casts Jesus in a favorable light.

The second observation indicating how sharply the crowd, in being well disposed toward Jesus, contrasts with its leaders concerns Jesus' activity. Twice, at the beginning and toward the end of his story, Mark contrasts the crowd with the religious authorities by juxtaposing a negative response to Jesus on the part of the authorities to a positive response on the part of the crowd. In Capernaum, some of the scribes charge Jesus with blasphemy for granting the paralytic forgiveness (2:6-7). The crowd, however, when it sees Jesus heal the paralytic, is amazed and glorifies God, saying, "We never saw anything like this!" (2:12). And after Jesus cleanses the temple in Jerusalem, Mark reports that the reaction of the chief priests and the scribes is to look for a way to destroy him (11:18). Of the crowd, however, Mark reports that it is astonished by Jesus' teaching, so much so that the authorities fear the crowd and take no action against Jesus (11:18).

Although the crowd is, on the one hand, well disposed toward Jesus and thus differs markedly from the religious authorities, it is, on the other hand, "without faith" in Jesus. John the Baptist readies the crowd for the coming of Jesus (1:4-5), but Jesus does not win the crowd over to his cause. The crowd may regard him as a prophet, but it also regards John as a prophet and does not see Jesus for the one he truly is, the Messiah Son of God. Because the place of the crowd is with those "outside," God does not impart to it the secret of his kingdom (4:10-11). Addressed by Jesus in parables, which he explains only to "insiders" like the disciples (4:33-34), the crowd cannot comprehend them. Despite the fact that the crowd reacts to Jesus' teaching and healing with amazement, or astonishment, this is an expression not of understanding but of incomprehension.[80] During Jesus' passion, the crowd at last casts its lot with the religious authorities and against Jesus. Though Jesus has taught the crowd daily in the temple, it accompanies Judas with swords and clubs to arrest Jesus.[81] At Jesus' hearing before Pilate, the crowd cries out for the release of Barabbas and insists on Jesus' crucifixion

(15:11-14). In fact, it is to satisfy the crowd that Pilate delivers Jesus to the soldiers to be crucified (15:15). Finally, as Jesus hangs on the cross the crowd, in the persons of the passers-by, blasphemes him, so that in the last scene in which it appears, the crowd demonstrates its complete solidarity with its leaders (15:29-30).

To recapitulate, the crowd in Mark's story is at once "well disposed" toward Jesus and "without faith" in him. In being well disposed toward Jesus, the crowd stands in contrast to its leaders, the religious authorities. In being without faith in Jesus, the crowd stands in contrast to the disciples.

Minor Characters

Thus far, we have discussed the major characters in Mark's story: Jesus, who is the protagonist; the religious authorities, who are the antagonists; and identifiable groups like the disciples or the crowd who appear throughout the story. To do a more exhaustive study of characterization, one could also treat other figures, such as John the Baptist, Herod Antipas, and Pilate.

Besides all of these, however, there is a host of minor characters who populate the world of Mark's story.[82] These characters appear suddenly and then vanish, never to be seen again. Some bear names or other identifying designations, like "Jairus" or "Simon's mother-in-law," but most do not. The roles these characters play vary so greatly that it is not immediately obvious whether certain ones exhibit traits at all. (*a*) Some minor characters are so unobtrusive in the episode in which they appear that they virtually meld with the setting, or scenery. For example, the only thing Mark reports concerning Simon the leper is that it is in his house at Bethany that the woman comes and anoints Jesus' head (14:3). (*b*) Other minor characters tend only to facilitate the action of an episode. A striking case in point is Herodias's daughter. Her dancing enables Herodias to maneuver vain and foolish Herod Antipas into ordering the beheading of John the Baptist (6:14-29). (*c*) Still other minor characters serve mainly as catalysts, which is to say that they provide opportunity for other characters to exhibit the traits they possess. The man with the withered hand whom Jesus heals on the sabbath provides the opportunity for Jesus to "do good" on the sabbath and for the Pharisees to "do evil," even plotting Jesus' death (3:1-6).

There are numerous minor characters, however, whose role or status does enable them to exhibit one or more traits. These traits are, for the most part, positive in nature, though not always. The underlings of the Sanhedrin take control of Jesus "with blows" (14:65); the Roman soldiers scourge him, mock him, strip him, and crucify him (15:15-26); and Barabbas, in contrast to Jesus, is said to be a murderer and revolutionary (15:7). Still, of the various traits the minor characters exhibit, two especially catch the reader's eye and each one is exemplified by its own cast of characters. First, there are those minor characters who stand out because they exhibit "faith," or "trust," in Jesus. And second, there are those who stand out because they somehow convey, by who they are or what they do, what it means to "serve."

The importance of these two groups is that, like most minor characters, they function as "foils"[83] ("contrasts") for certain of the major characters. Consider, for example, the disciples, the religious authorities, and the crowd on the matter of faith, or trust, in Jesus. The disciples start off well, but the farther the story progresses, the more benighted they become, until at last they break their pledge of allegiance to Jesus and apostatize. The religious authorities never place trust in Jesus; just the opposite, they are implacably opposed to him throughout. And the crowd as such, although it proves to be well disposed toward Jesus, never joins itself to him in a bond of trust and, toward the end, turns against him.

In stark contrast to the latter, Mark punctuates the greater part of his story with a string of minor characters all of whom do evince great faith, or trust, in Jesus. Those belonging to this group are, for example, the leper who approaches Jesus to be cleansed (1:40-45); those who bring the paralytic to Jesus for healing (2:3-5); Jairus, who pleads with Jesus for the life of his daughter (5:21-24, 35-43); the woman with the hemorrhage who touches Jesus' garment in the confidence she will be healed (5:25-34); the Syrophoenician woman who calls upon Jesus to drive the demon out of her daughter (7:25-30); the father who brings his son to Jesus to have an unclean spirit cast out (9:14-29); and blind Bartimaeus, who shouts aloud to Jesus to have mercy on him (10:46-52).[84] Typically, these persons approach Jesus in the firm belief that he possesses the divine authority to do as they ask. Note in this connection the words of the leper, "If you will, you can make me clean!" (1:40). Most often, obstacles stand in their way, but so strong is their faith that they surmount them. The Syrophoenician woman, for instance, must overcome the major liability of being a gentile (7:25-30). And without exception, Jesus shows all these persons that he is graciously disposed toward them by granting them their requests. As dynamic models of faith, these various minor characters contrast pointedly with the disciples, the religious authorities, and the crowd.

The second group of minor characters referred to functions more specifically as a foil for the disciples. These characters appear in the long end section of Mark's story and especially in the passion narrative (8:27—16:8). They exemplify, by who they are or what they do, what it means to "serve." In the person of Peter, the disciples reject the notion of servanthood (8:31-37). They "think the things not of God, but of humans," which reveals that they would prefer to "gain the world" (8:33, 36). As a result, they demonstrate on the way to Jerusalem that they are enamored of status (9:33-34), wealth (10:23-27), and positions of power (10:35-41). As a counterexample to the disciples' desire for status, Jesus singles out children: Children are without status and have great need to be served.[85] As an example of the danger that wealth poses for disciples, the rich man demonstrates that having great possessions threatens to make discipleship impossible (10:17-22). And as a counterexample to the disciples' desire for positions of power, Jesus points first to himself (10:42-45) and, later, to a poor widow: Her devotion to God is so great that, having put in the temple treasury all the money she has, she lives in total dependence on him (12:41-44).

To turn to the passion narrative, any number of minor characters function as foils for the disciples in that they serve Jesus in a way the disciples should do but do not.[86] Thus, the woman in the house of Simon the leper anoints Jesus' body for burial (14:3-9). Simon of Cyrene, in carrying the cross of Jesus, acts out the very word that Jesus earlier directed to the disciples (15:21; 8:34). The centurion, who is "converted" by observing Jesus die, is the first human to affirm publicly the divine sonship of Jesus (15:39). The women watching the crucifixion from afar are the ones who have not only ministered to Jesus in life but have also followed him from Galilee all the way to the cross (15:40-41). Joseph of Arimathea[87] becomes the one who musters the courage to emulate what John the Baptist's disciples earlier did for their master: Joseph goes to Pilate, secures the corpse of Jesus, and lays it in its tomb (6:29; 15:42-46). And the three women, not knowing that Jesus has already been anointed for burial in the house of Simon the leper, come to the tomb with the intention of anointing his body (16:1).

The minor characters, then, are individuals or persons of many stripes. While their roles are varied, they function in the main as foils for certain of the major characters. They make their greatest impact upon Mark's story as two broad groups that either exhibit great "faith" in Jesus or somehow exemplify what it is to "serve."

Plot

The final feature of Mark's story that calls for comment is its plot. The plot of a story has to do with the way the events are arranged. Events occur not haphazardly but in a carefully ordered sequence. This sequence is governed by time and causality so as to reach an overall climax and to elicit from the reader some desired response.[88] In the case of Mark's story, the plot has a beginning (1:1-13), a middle (1:14—8:26), and an end (8:27—16:8). Not untypically, the force driving the story forward is the element of conflict.[89] In Jesus' death and resurrection, the conflict of the story comes to fundamental resolution. In Jesus' Parousia, it will come to final resolution. The response the story would elicit from the reader is that the reader be a disciple of Jesus as shaped by his or her reading or hearing of the story. What this means ultimately is best said by Jesus himself: "If anyone would come after me, let him deny himself and take up his cross, and let him follow me! For whoever would save his life will lose it; and whoever loses his life for my sake and the gospel's will save it."

At the center of the conflict of Mark's story is Jesus. His struggle is, on the one hand, with Israel (the religious authorities and the crowd) and, on the other hand, with the disciples. The nature of each struggle is intrinsically different.

Jesus' struggle with the disciples, who have joined themselves to him in a pledge of total allegiance, is to overcome their ignorance concerning who he is, what he is about, and what the true meaning of discipleship is. By contrast, Jesus' struggle with Israel is to bring it to receive him as the supreme agent whom God has sent and in whom God in his end-time rule graciously draws near to humankind. Whereas Jesus' struggle with the disciples leads first to failure but ultimately, as can be projected, to reconciliation, his struggle with Israel leads inescapably to crucifixion. Israel refuses to receive Jesus as God's supreme agent, and the authorities are successful in their conspiracy to have him put to death. Despite this, Jesus' death is not portrayed as the violent end of a failed ministry. Ironically, God and Jesus too will the death of Jesus: to establish a new covenant wherein there is atonement for sins and salvation for all humankind. As a sign that Jesus' death does not symbolize destruction at the hands of his enemies, God resurrects him and exalts him to universal rule. In so doing, God puts him in the right in his struggle with Israel and thus vindicates him. In the time following Jesus' resurrection and leading up to the end of history, disciples of Jesus will proclaim to all nations the good news of the salvation

God has accomplished in him. Then, at the end, the risen, exalted, and vindicated Jesus will, with great power and glory, return to earth in the sight of all, even his enemies, to usher in the consummated rule of God.

This brief overview of the conflict around which the plot of Mark's story revolves indicates that intertwined in Mark are three primary story lines and one secondary story line. Leaving aside the story line of the crowd as secondary, the primary story lines are the respective stories of Jesus, of the religious authorities, and of the disciples. The way we shall deal with Mark's larger story, then, is by treating each of these story lines, beginning with that of Jesus.

2

The Story of
JESUS

s the protagonist, Jesus[1] dominates Mark's story. Virtually without exception, the spotlight remains trained on him.[2] In the beginning of the story, Mark presents Jesus to the reader (1:1-13). In the middle, he tells of Jesus' public ministry to Israel (1:14—8:26). And in the long end section, he tells of Jesus' journey to Jerusalem and his suffering, death, and rising (8:27—16:8).

The Presentation of Jesus

Mark uses the beginning of his story (1:1-13) to set the stage. At the head of this story, he places a caption and a long quotation from the Old Testament. The caption reads, "The beginning of the gospel of Jesus Christ, the Son of God" (1:1).[3] In this caption three things leap out. The first thing has to do with the term "beginning." In Mark's view, the whole of the story of Jesus he is about to narrate constitutes only the beginning, or foundational, part of a longer story not yet finished. While this beginning part will conclude with the resurrection and be proclaimed following Easter,[4] the longer story of Jesus will continue until such time as he returns in splendor at the close of the age. The second thing concerns the term "gospel." In Mark's perspective, the story of Jesus is itself of the nature of gospel, or "good news": In his Son

Jesus, God in his end-time rule has drawn near to save humankind (Israel and the gentiles).[5] And the third thing is that the good news of Mark's story is bound up with the protagonist of his story, who is "Jesus Christ, the Son of God." In so identifying Jesus, Mark raises a claim on his behalf: Jesus of Nazareth is the Christ (Israel's anointed King, the Messiah), God's royal Son. As such, Jesus is God's supreme agent in whom God is decisively at work.

Technically, the quotation from the OT (1:2-3) introduces Mark's brief account of the ministry of John the Baptist.[6] More broadly, however, it also conveys in capsule form the content of Mark's story. Since the quotation itself attests to the fulfillment of divine prophecy, it indicates that the events comprising Mark's story will all belong to the fullness of time, which is the time of the gospel. Moreover, these events will also take place under the direct governance of God and constitute the sending of John the Baptist and Jesus: "Behold, I [God] send my messenger [John] before you [Jesus])" (1:2). God himself is the one who initiates and guides the action that will take place in the ministries of John and Jesus. The references to John ("my messenger") and Jesus ("you") stand as ciphers for their ministries. Mark's story, therefore, will tell of the ministries of John and Jesus, and both John and Jesus will come as the agents of God acting on the authority of God. Also, since John is but the messenger who precedes Jesus, Mark's story will focus primarily on Jesus, God's supreme agent.

The Figure and Ministry of John

In line with the OT quotation in 1:2-3, Mark next plunges directly into his story. He sketches the figure and ministry of John and also presents him as describing his relationship to Jesus (1:4-8).

John appears in the desert of Judea near the Jordan River (1:4-5), fulfilling the hope of a new exodus (1:3).[7] Although eating locusts and wild honey is simply characteristic of persons inhabiting the desert (1:6), John's clothing (especially the leather belt) identifies him with the prophet Elijah (2 Kings 1:8). As the latter-day Elijah, John fulfills the end-time expectations associated with Elijah by "restoring all things" (9:12). Specifically, John proclaims a baptism of repentance for the forgiveness of sins and receives the people of Judea and all the Jerusalemites who come out to him, submit to his baptism, and confess their sins (1:4-5). In so doing, John readies Israel for the arrival of his successor.

In looking to the coming of his successor, John prophesies concerning him (1:7-8). He calls him the "mightier One" and contrasts his own baptism with the "baptism" of that one. His own baptism aims at preparing Israel for the coming of the mightier One by summoning it to repentance. The "baptism" the mightier One will perform is the ministry he will discharge. Through his ministry, the mightier One will bestow the Holy Spirit, which is to say that he will be the one who accomplishes final salvation.

In Mark's story, then, John is the "forerunner" of Jesus who readies Israel for Jesus' coming. As forerunner, however, John is more than merely the temporal predecessor of Jesus. Indeed, in his own person and fate he foreshadows the person and fate of Jesus. To illustrate, both John and Jesus are sent by God in fulfillment of OT prophecy (1:2-3). As end-time agents of God, both discharge their ministries in the time of the gospel. Both proclaim a message summoning Israel to repentance.[8] Both gather disciples.[9] Both attract huge throngs of people (1:5; 3:7-8).[10] Both utter words of prophecy (1:7-8).[11] Both are repudiated by the religious authorities of Israel.[12] Both are delivered up to their enemies.[13] And both die unjustly and disgracefully at the hands of rulers who permit themselves to be manipulated by others.[14] To know of John is to know in advance of Jesus.

The Figure of Jesus

True to John's prophecy, Jesus arrives on the scene virtually at once (1:9). He too is baptized by John in the Jordan River. Immediately thereafter, Jesus goes up from the water and consequently removes himself from John (1:10). In private encounter with God, he becomes the recipient of two reve- latory events (1:10-11). In the first event, which is visual, Jesus sees the heavens split apart and the Spirit descend upon him as a dove (1:10). In this act, God endows Jesus with his Spirit and empowers him for the ministry he is about to begin. In the second event, which is auditory, Jesus hears God himself address him: "You are my beloved Son, in you I take delight!" (1:11).

The words God speaks constitute a composite quotation drawn from Ps. 2:7; Isa. 42:1; and Gen. 22:2. In Isa. 42:1, the servant in whom God delights is one whom God has "chosen" for ministry. In Gen. 22:2, Abraham's beloved son Isaac is his "only" son. And in Psalm 2, God is described as solemnly addressing the words "My son are you" to his "anointed" ("messiah") from the royal house of David.[15] With- in the context of Mark's story, God's words to Jesus become a solemn affirmation that he, the Messiah-King from the line of David, is God's only, or unique, Son whom God has chosen for end-time ministry.

In these two revelatory events, Mark brings the beginning of his story to its culmination. In addressing Jesus, God him- self in effect presents Jesus to the reader. God himself enters the world of Mark's story and makes known how he under- stands Jesus' identity. Since God in Mark's story is the supreme ruler of the universe and all history, the reader recognizes that God's understanding of Jesus' identity is normative.[16] This means that as the reader moves through Mark's story, he or she henceforth has a measuring rod by which to judge the understanding of Jesus' identity that other characters will express. The extent to which any character's understanding of Jesus' identity coincides with or diverges from God's un- derstanding, will reflect the extent to which it is right or wrong, true or false.

By depicting God as having empowered Jesus with his Spir- it, Mark likewise informs the reader of what it means for Jesus to be God's Son. It means that Jesus has a unique filial re- lationship to God and is therefore God's supreme agent of salvation. In Jesus, God is present and decisively at work; what Jesus says and does, he says and does on the direct authority of God. Also, Jesus is utterly obedient to God; he loves God with heart, soul, mind, and strength, so that he alone is "qualified" to accomplish salvation. To be sure, God is said in Mark's story to be the "Father" not only of Jesus but also of the disciples (11:25). Never, however, is anyone except Jesus ever said to be "the Son of God." Jesus' divine sonship is unique.

After Jesus has been endowed with the Spirit and God's voice has sounded from heaven, the Spirit drives him into the desert to be put to the test by Satan (1:12-13). If heaven is the abode of God, the desert is the abode of Satan. Just as Israel, who was also God's son (Exod. 4:22-23), spent forty years in the desert, so Jesus Son of God spends forty days in the desert. In testing Jesus, Satan endeavors to entice him to break faith with God and thus forfeit both his sonship and his authority. Jesus, however, withstands Satan. This is strongly alluded to by the cryptic comment that he was "with the wild animals." This comment echoes passages from OT and Jewish literature that picture the future time of salvation as an era in which humans and wild beasts will once again live in peace with one another.[17] The presence of angels to sustain Jesus underlines the cosmic dimension of the temptation: Jesus' struggle with Satan is a clash between the kingdom of God and the kingdom of evil. In the temptation, then, Jesus Son of God shows what his ministry will be about: the binding of Satan and the inauguration of the end-time age of salvation (3:27).

Accordingly, in the beginning of his story (1:1-13) Mark presents John and especially Jesus to the reader and also tells of John's ministry. John is the forerunner of Jesus, and he accomplishes his task by readying Israel for the coming of Jesus (1:2-8). As Jesus' forerunner, John reflects in his person and fate the person and fate of Jesus. Immediately following John's prophecy of Jesus, Jesus arrives on the scene. In the accounts of his baptism and temptation (1:9-13), the beginning of Mark's story reaches its climax. The baptism picks up on the caption that Mark places at the head of his story and informs the reader of how God understands Jesus. As the reader looks on, God empowers Jesus with his Spirit, endowing him with divine authority, and solemnly affirms Jesus to be his royal Son. Then, led by the Spirit out into the desert, Jesus, God's powerful Son, successfully withstands the assault of Satan and reveals thereby that God has sent him to inaugurate the end-time age of salvation.

The Ministry of Jesus in and around Galilee

Mark next tells of Jesus' ministry in and around Galilee. The change in setting from the Jordan to Galilee signals a major turning point in the story. The beginning (1:1-13) gives way to the middle (1:14—8:26). In the beginning, Jesus is presented to the reader and, except for the notation that "he came" from Nazareth (1:8), is passive rather than active: Mark himself asserts his identity (1:1); scripture says he is sent by God (1:2-3); his imminent appearance is prophesied by John (1:7-8); he is baptized by John (1:9); he is empowered with the Spirit by God and declared by God to be his Son (1:10-11); and he is cast out into the desert by the Spirit, where he is put to the test by Satan and served by angels (1:12-13). The moment John's public activity ends with his arrest, however, Jesus commences his ministry to Israel (1:14). No longer passive, he engages in a whirl of activity.

The Public Activity of Jesus

Mark documents the itinerant ministry that Jesus undertakes throughout Galilee and beyond with numerous summary passages.[18] As Mark points out, Jesus proclaims the gospel of God, announcing that the fullness of time and God's drawing near in his rule are a summons to people to repent and to place their trust in the good news he bears (1:14-15, 38-39). He calls disciples to follow him and be with him, and he creates the special circle of the twelve.[19] He teaches with incomparable authority about God's rule and will in the synagogues and throughout all Galilee, and the people are astounded at his teaching (1:21-22).[20] He heals great numbers of people afflicted with many kinds of diseases so that huge crowds, hearing of his mighty deeds, throng to him to have him touch and save the sick.[21] And he exorcises demons, thus plundering the house of the strong man Satan by releasing persons from his power.[22] As a result of Jesus' vigorous activity of preaching, teaching, healing, and exorcising demons, he creates no little stir among the people of Galilee, and his fame spreads far and wide. Typically, Jesus amazes or astonishes hearers or onlookers.[23] People not only in Galilee but also in other parts of Palestine and even in gentile lands hear of him, to wit: Judea, Jerusalem, Idumea, Transjordan, Tyre and Sidon, and the Decapolis (3:7-8; 5:20). So great is his fame, in fact, that it cannot be suppressed. For example, Jesus can command silence after performing a miracle, and yet his command will be ignored and the news of him proclaimed (1:44-45; 7:36). The upshot is that wherever Jesus appears, in city, village, countryside, or beside the sea, people stream to him[24] and the crowd follows him.[25] At times, the crowd becomes burdensome or even dangerous, so that Jesus temporarily withdraws or attempts to escape by boat.[26]

Human Ignorance concerning Jesus' Identity

Given the widespread activity and fame of Jesus, one is tempted to think that his identity would be a secret to no one. The opposite, however, is the case. Mark takes pains to show that none of the human characters in the middle of his story—neither the people nor their leaders nor the disciples nor Jesus' family, relatives, or acquaintances—knows his identity. In this respect, the middle of Mark's story is the same as the beginning. In the beginning too, the human characters have no knowledge of Jesus' identity. The people of Judea and Jerusalem who hear John's message and go out to him for baptism do not return having learned who Jesus is. As John speaks to them of the mightier One to come, they understand only that this figure will be more powerful than John (1:5, 7). To be more powerful than John, however, could mean no more than being another, albeit greater, prophet (6:14-16). It is the reader, not the people, who is privy to the real truth: that being the mightier One means being the Son of God. Indeed, one must doubt that John himself is to be regarded as fully appreciating what it will mean for Jesus to be the mightier One. Jesus' empowerment with the Spirit and God's affirmation of Jesus' divine sonship do not occur in the presence of John. They occur only after Jesus has gone up from the water and removed himself from John (1:10a). This explains why Jesus alone sees the heavens split apart and the Spirit descend ("he saw," 1:10). It also explains why the words God utters are addressed to Jesus exclusively ("You are my beloved Son, in you I take delight!" 1:11).

If Mark refuses knowledge of Jesus' identity to human characters in the beginning and middle of his story, who, then, knows of his identity? The answer is Mark himself as narrator, the reader, and such supernatural beings as God, Satan, and demons. In the middle of Mark's story, the demons regularly and publicly shout aloud the truth that Jesus is the Son of God (3:11).[27] Despite this, Mark forbids the reader to imagine that their shouts ever reach the ears of humans. On the contrary, these shouts are either suppressed by Jesus[28] or occur in a place where they cannot be heard (5:2-12).

From a literary standpoint, the shouts of the demons in reality occur not for the benefit of any character in Mark's story but for the benefit of the reader. In Mark's perspective, Jesus can properly be called by several titles, chief of which are "Messiah," "King of the Jews [Israel]," "Son of David," and "Son of God." While all of these titles are correct, they are not all of equal significance. "Son of God" is the preeminent title for Jesus. It constitutes the way God "thinks" about him and points directly to the unique filial relationship he has to God. So as not to permit the reader to forget that Jesus is God's Son, Mark has the demons shout this aloud. Although these shouts are not heard by human characters within the story, they are heard by the reader.

Overall, Mark employs a literary pattern to deal with the theme of Jesus' identity in the middle of his story (1:14—8:26). This pattern is "contrapuntal" in nature.[29] On the one hand, the demons, as supernatural beings, know that Jesus is the Son of God (1:34; 3:11). This is the ultimate secret of his identity, as uttered by God (1:11). On the other hand, human characters in the story have no inkling of this secret. Confronted by Jesus' mighty words and deeds, they respond uncomprehendingly by continually asking who he is. What results is the following contrapuntal pattern: Demonic shouts that Jesus is the Son of God alternate with the questions human characters pose about who Jesus could conceivably be.[30] By making use of this pattern, Mark juxtaposes "supernatural knowledge" and "human ignorance." Concretely, the questions that various characters pose by way of responding to some act of Jesus illustrate this phenomenon of human ignorance about his identity. In the synagogue at Capernaum (1:21-28), Jesus, having taught the people, encounters a man with an unclean spirit. He demonstrates his power over the spirit by suppressing its recognition of him and exorcising it. Having been astounded at Jesus' teaching, the people are equally astounded at the exorcism. In amazement, they both query one another and exclaim, "What is this? A new teaching with authority?" (1:27).

On the surface, this double question appears to have little to do with the matter of Jesus' identity. It envisages the exorcism Jesus has just performed and makes mention of his teaching. Still, inquiry about Jesus' exorcism is also inquiry about Jesus himself. This is clear from the remaining words the people utter and from the narrative comment that Mark too makes: The people continue, "*He* commands even the unclean spirits, and they obey *him*"; and Mark comments, "And at once the report of *him* spread everywhere" (1:27-28). Accordingly, implicit in the question "What is this?" is the question "Who is this?" The people in the synagogue at Capernaum are astounded at the authority with which Jesus teaches and acts and this causes them to wonder who he is.

The second question having to do with Jesus' identity stems from some of the scribes (2:1-12). Jesus is at home in Capernaum proclaiming the word to a crowd when four men carrying a paralytic on a pallet approach him. Unable to reach him, they climb to the roof, dig through the clay, and let the paralytic on the pallet down to him. Seeing the faith of these men, Jesus forgives the paralytic his sins. This, in turn, provokes the scribes sitting there to reason in their hearts, "Why does this man speak thus? He blasphemes! Who can forgive sins but God alone?" (2:7). Perceiving that these scribes harbor these thoughts in their hearts, Jesus addresses them openly. He replies to their questions by asserting that "the Son of man has authority on earth to forgive sins" (2:10).

Here too the issue of Jesus' identity is broached, but again indirectly. The scribes believe that no human has the authority to forgive sins. In asking, therefore, who can forgive sins, they are in effect asking who this Jesus is who dares to arrogate to himself the prerogative of God and forgive sins. In his reply to them, Jesus asserts with undisguised boldness that he, in fact, is "the man" who possesses the authority on earth to forgive sins and hence to do what otherwise only God can do.

The third question concerning the identity of Jesus stems from the disciples (4:35-41). Following his parable discourse from the boat, Jesus commands the disciples toward evening to set sail for the other side of the sea. On the way, as Jesus is asleep in the stern of the boat, the disciples become caught in a fierce storm. With the waves beating against the boat and filling it, they arouse Jesus and call on him to show his concern for them by rescuing them from their peril. In response to their appeal, Jesus rebukes the wind and commands the sea to silence. At once a great calm ensues. Overwhelmed, the disciples, cowardly, bereft of faith, and filled with fear, ask one another, "Who then is this, that even wind and sea obey him?" (4:41).

The fourth question touching on the identity of Jesus occurs in the mouths of the villagers of Nazareth (6:1-6). Accompanied by his disciples, Jesus travels to his hometown. On the day of the sabbath, he enters the synagogue and teaches, with acquaintances, relatives, and family in attendance. When the many people assembled hear him, they become astonished and fall to asking one another about the wisdom he exhibits and the great miracles he reputedly performs. The motive sparking their questions, however, is unbelief. They find it incredible that one whose origins they know should be able to do such things. Taking offense at Jesus, they ask themselves, "Is not this the carpenter, the son of Mary?" (6:3).

With this question, Mark suddenly breaks off the string of inquiries about the identity of Jesus stretching from the beginning of his ministry to his rejection here in Nazareth. Abruptly, Mark exploits instead the theme of the fame of Jesus. Jesus' fame has caused the Jewish public to wonder and speculate about who he might be.

As Mark tells it, Jesus, having left Nazareth, sends the disciples out on their ministry to Israel (6:7-13). While they are away, Mark interrupts his story of Jesus to recount for the reader the fate already befallen John the Baptist (6:14-29). As a preface to this account, Mark presents a survey of Jewish public opinion concerning Jesus (6:14-16). Because Jesus' name has become known, speculation about who he is has reached the court of King Herod (Antipas). The reports that Herod hears, however, are mixed. Some people, for example, claim that Jesus is John the Baptist raised from the dead. Others insist that he is Elijah. And still others contend that he is a prophet, like one of the prophets of old. For his part, Herod opts for the first view: "John, whom I beheaded, has been raised" (6:16).

What is the reader to make of these views of the Jewish public and Herod? For one thing, they are all related in the sense that in all of them Jesus is understood to be a prophet of some sort. For another thing, they are all false. They are false because they conflict with reliable information already given the reader. The reader knows that Jesus is not John the Baptist come back to life, for John was the forerunner of Jesus. Nor can Jesus be Elijah, for John was the one who fulfilled the end-time expectations associated with Elijah. Nor can Jesus be another of the prophets of old, for their task, the reader has learned, is to foretell of the time of Jesus (1:2). No, the perceptions of the Jewish public and Herod evince no true insight into the identity of Jesus.

To recapitulate, in the middle of his story (1:14—8:26) Mark describes Jesus' public ministry in and around Galilee. If Jesus is passive in the beginning, in the middle he embarks on a widespread ministry of preaching, calling disciples, teaching, healing, and exorcising demons. As the Son of God in whom God in his end-time rule has drawn near, Jesus summons Israel to repent and to believe in the good news. Because he is powerful in word and deed, his fame goes out. Humans, however, do not know who he is. True, demons shout aloud that he is the Son of God, but their shouts are suppressed or not heard. In the face of Jesus' mighty acts, all segments of Israel—people, leaders, disciples, and Jesus' family, relatives, and acquaintances—ask uncomprehendingly who he is. After a time, speculation about his identity surfaces among the public. Various segments believe him to be a prophet of some sort. This view of him, however, is false. It coincides neither with the view Mark has expressed nor with the view expressed by God.

The Journey of Jesus to Jerusalem and His Suffering, Death, and Resurrection

In the long end section of his story (8:27—16:8), Mark tells of Jesus' journey to Jerusalem and of his suffering, death, and resurrection. The terse comment that Jesus and the disciples are now "on the way"[31] that will take them to Jerusalem directs attention to the second major turning point in the story (8:27). The goal of this "way" is set forth in the three passion predictions: "Behold, we are going up to Jerusalem, and the Son of man will be delivered to the chief priests and the scribes . . . [and] to the Gentiles" (10:33; 8:31; 9:31). The climax of the story and the resolution of Jesus' conflict with Israel occur in the account of Jesus' suffering and resurrection (chaps. 14–16).

Mark so narrates the story of Jesus that the themes of Jesus' identity and destiny are intertwined. Not until a human knows what Jesus is about, death on the cross, does a human know who Jesus is. Similarly, not until a human knows who Jesus is, the Son of God, does a human know what Jesus is about. The result is that by pursuing the theme of Jesus' identity, one can at the same time pursue the theme of Jesus' destiny.

In comparison with the middle of his story, Mark dramatically alters the way he deals with the theme of Jesus' identity in the end section. In the middle, demons shout aloud that Jesus is the Son of God, but humans only wonder and speculate about who he might be. The guess that he is a prophet of some sort is mistaken. In the end section, however, demons no longer shout aloud Jesus' identity. Instead, those focusing on this issue with newfound intensity are humans, and some evince insight into it. Indeed, Jesus' identity is progressively unveiled in three stages, though only from the standpoint of the reader. It is to these three stages that we now turn.

Jesus the Messiah

The first stage in the progressive disclosure of Jesus' identity is the confession of Peter on behalf of the disciples (8:27-30). In the regions of Caesarea Philippi, Jesus himself suddenly broaches the question of his identity and asks the disciples who the Jewish public ("men") says he is. In answer, the disciples merely repeat the rumors Herod Antipas too had heard: Jesus is John the Baptist, Elijah, or one of the prophets (8:28; 6:14-15). Ignoring these responses, Jesus asks the disciples who they say he is. In reply, Peter declares, "You are the Messiah [Christ]!" (8:29). In turn, Jesus commands all the disciples to silence (8:30).

Peter's reply is correct but insufficient. On the one hand, it is correct. It is correct first of all because it agrees with the caption with which Mark began his story ("Jesus [is the] Christ"; 1:1). Second, it is also correct because it encapsulates the way the disciples, in contradistinction to the Jewish public, have come to understand Jesus since first called.[32] Specifically, they have witnessed him authoritatively preach, teach, heal, and exorcise demons. In fact, they themselves, on the authority Jesus gave them, have engaged in the selfsame activities.[33] Accordingly, in declaring Jesus to be the Messiah, Peter is in effect confessing Jesus to be Israel's anointed King sent by God to preach, teach, heal, and exorcise demons. As is apparent from Mark's story, this is, again, correct.

On the other hand, Peter's confession is also insufficient. It is insufficient because it communicates too little about either the identity or the destiny of Jesus. It communicates too little about Jesus' identity because it describes him more generally as Israel's Anointed King. To be sure, Jesus is indeed Israel's Anointed King. As Jesus hangs upon the cross, the religious authorities mock him by addressing him as "the Messiah, the King of Israel" (15:32). The irony of this scene is that in so mocking Jesus, the authorities are unwittingly speaking the truth. Still, what sets Jesus apart from all other anointed kings of Israel is, above all, the uniqueness of his filial relationship to God. To emphasize this, both Mark as narrator and especially God define the general title Messiah more narrowly in terms of the title Son of God (1:1, 11; also 14:61).

In similar fashion, Peter's confession likewise communicates too little about Jesus' destiny. It envisages neither his suffering nor death. At 8:31, Jesus teaches the disciples for the first time that it is God's will that he suffer and be killed. As spokesman for the disciples, Peter repudiates Jesus' teaching (8:32). Jesus in turn reprimands Peter and indicates that his rebuff is for the others as well by fixing his gaze on all (8:33). Thus, while Peter's confession correctly envisages Jesus as God's authoritative preacher, gatherer of disciples, teacher, healer, and exorcist, it makes no allusion whatever to his passion.

Because Peter's confession, though correct, is insufficient, Jesus commands the disciples to silence about his identity (8:30). Until the disciples comprehend that suffering and death are part and parcel of his destiny, they will not fully comprehend his identity.

The pericope on the transfiguration confirms this observation (9:2-10). Atop the mountain, Jesus appears in transfigured splendor before Peter, James, and John. From a cloud, God's voice sounds for a second time within the world of Mark's story: "This is my beloved Son, hear him!" (9:7). The declaration "This is my beloved Son" echoes the words God spoke following the baptism and affirm once again that Jesus is God's unique Son. The exhortation "hear him!" enjoins the three disciples to listen to Jesus when he teaches them, as he did in the first passion prediction, that at the heart of his ministry lie suffering and death. Filled with fear, Peter and the two brothers fail to grasp the revelation they receive (9:5-6). As they descend from the mountain, Jesus commands the three to say nothing to anyone about their experience until after the resurrection (9:9). This command signals the reader that, until the resurrection, the disciples can be expected to comprehend neither the deepest secret about Jesus' identity nor the central truth about his destiny.

Jesus the Son of David

The second stage in the progressive disclosure of Jesus' identity centers on his Davidic sonship (10:46—11:11; 12:35-37). Outside Jericho, Bartimaeus, a blind beggar, hears that Jesus of Nazareth passes by. In great faith, he cries out to Jesus as the Son of David and bids him to grant him the gift of his sight. Although many in the crowd would hush Bartimaeus, Jesus summons him, asks him what he would have him do, and then dismisses him with a healing word that acknowledges his faith.

What is noteworthy in this scene is that Bartimaeus, a person of great faith, appeals to Jesus as the Son of David. By granting Bartimaeus his request for sight, Jesus in effect accepts for himself the title Son of David. Moreover, he also shows how he fulfills the end-time expectations associated with David. He does so not by donning the helmet of a warrior king but by using his authority to heal and in this way to save.

Bartimaeus joins the crowd following Jesus into Jerusalem (11:1-11). As Jesus approaches the city, those accompanying him hail him as the bearer of "the coming kingdom of our father David" (11:11). Once again, Jesus stands before the reader as the Son of David. Also, the animal on which he rides is not a steed of war but a colt or "messianic mount" (Zech. 9:9). Jesus Son of David is the humble king of peace.

As in the case of "Messiah," so "Son of David" too is a correct but insufficient title for Jesus. To make this point, Mark narrates the pericope on the question about David's son (12:35-37). While teaching the crowd in the temple, Jesus poses a question of antinomy: How can the Messiah simultaneously be both the son and the lord of David? This question is antinomous because it contains within it two ostensibly contradictory views about the Messiah: If said to be the son of David, the Messiah is characterized merely as the descendant of David and in this sense less than David. If said to be the lord of David, the Messiah is characterized as greater than David. The conundrum, then, is this: How can the Messiah at the same time be both less than David and greater than David? While Jesus leaves the answer to be inferred, the reader can readily supply it: The Messiah is the son of David because he stands in the line of David; the Messiah is at the same time the lord of David because, as the Son of God,[34] he is of higher station and authority than David. Applied to Jesus himself, the answer Jesus' question anticipates points to the claim that Mark would make on Jesus' behalf: In his story, Jesus Messiah is in fact the descendant of David and hence the Son of David; still, he is also more than merely Son of David because he is the Son of God (1:11; 9:7).

Jesus the Son of God

Events in the Temple.   The third stage in the progressive disclosure of Jesus' identity focuses on the secret that he is the Son of God. Though not immediately apparent, this stage begins already with Jesus' arrival in Jerusalem (11:11). Seemingly, this takes place on the Sunday preceding Jesus' death and resurrection, and time in Mark's story slows to days.[35] Upon entering Jerusalem, Jesus proceeds directly to the temple to look around (11:11). This done, he retires to Bethany for the night. Next day, he returns to the temple and at once cleanses it, throwing the sacrificial system into disarray (11:15-18). With this utterly provocative act, Jesus challenges the rule of the chief priests and the scribes in the central place of their authority and threatens to undermine their position and power. Indeed, he incites the chief priests and the scribes to look for a way to destroy him (11:18).

On the day following the cleansing, Jesus is again in the temple. Joined by the elders, the chief priests and the scribes confront him and demand to know who it is who authorized him to do "these things" (11:27-28). In response, Jesus tells them that he will answer their question if they will first answer his, to wit: "Was the baptism of John from heaven [God] or from men?" (11:30). Trapped, the authorities refuse to answer (11:33). Should they grant that John discharged his ministry of baptism on the authority of God, they would then need to explain why they repudiated him (11:31). Should they insist that John discharged his ministry on purely human authority, they would place themselves at odds with the crowd, which holds John to have been a prophet sent by God (11:32). Since they give Jesus no answer, neither does he give them any answer (11:33). The reader, however, knows the answer to their question: The one on whose authority Jesus acts is God himself (1:10-11).

This controversy over Jesus' authority sets the stage for his narration of the parable of the wicked husbandmen (12:1-12). In this parable Jesus, still addressing the chief priests, scribes, and elders, sketches God's dealings with Israel throughout the history of salvation. He identifies the owner of the vineyard with God, himself with the son of the owner of the vineyard, and the wicked tenant farmers, who kill the owner's son, with them. By means of these identifications, Jesus raises a bold claim concerning both himself and them. Concerning himself, his claim is that he is, in God's own eyes, the Son whom God has sent Israel (12:6). Concerning them, his claim is that they, like the wicked tenant farmers, have murder in their hearts and will kill him (12:7-8). Because the authorities understand Jesus' claims, their impulse is to arrest him on the spot (12:12). Still, they hold back for fear of the crowd.

The irony surrounding Jesus' narration of this parable is palpable. Although the religious authorities grasp Jesus' claim to be the Son of God with their minds, they reject it with their hearts.[36] Yet, in rejecting Jesus' claim, they are unwittingly rejecting the very claim God made on Jesus' behalf following the baptism and at the transfiguration.[37] Without recognizing it, they have made themselves opponents of God. Then too, in refusing to acknowledge that Jesus is the Son of God, they show that they remain ignorant of the secret of his identity. Jesus has told them who he is, but they have spurned his word. The secret of his identity remains unbroken.

Jesus' cleansing of the temple, the controversy over his authority, and Jesus' narration of the parable of the wicked husbandmen all spark further controversies in the temple (12:13-34). Pharisees and Herodians attempt to ensnare him in his speech (12:13-17) and Sadducees to confound him on the question of the resurrection (12:18-27). But for naught. Singly or in groups, all the parties that together make up the larger body of the religious authorities have directly challenged Jesus, but he has reduced them all to silence. As Mark reports, "And no one dared any longer to ask him any question" (12:34). In fact, in Jesus' last confrontation a "friendly scribe" openly acknowledges what Jesus has amply demonstrated: In his knowledge of the law and will of God, he is superior to all his opponents, for "he answered them well" (12:28-34). Having lost all courage to get the best of Jesus in debate, the authorities disappear from Mark's story and do not reappear until the opening scene of the passion account (14:1-2). For his part, Jesus turns first to the crowd, who hears his teaching gladly,[38] and then to the disciples, instructing them on love of God and total dependence on him and predicting events leading up to the Parousia.[39]

Events Surrounding the Passion.   Mark's story reaches its culmination in the passion account (chaps. 14–16).[40] Jesus' death is the point at which human understanding of both his identity and destiny finally becomes possible. It is also the point at which Jesus' conflict with Israel comes to fundamental resolution.

Mark dates the last week of Jesus' life from his entry into Jerusalem (11:1-11).[41] With the onset of Jesus' passion, the Passover and the Feast of Unleavened Bread[42] are now only "two days" off (14:1).[43] Apparently, then, it is Wednesday; on Thursday evening[44] Jesus will eat the last supper with the disciples, and on Friday he will die.[45] As Friday morning arrives and the death of Jesus approaches, Mark will slow time from days to hours.[46] Such slowing of time is yet another way of calling attention to the pivotal importance of Jesus' death.

In the opening scene of the passion, Mark reminds the reader who the key players are: Jesus and the religious authorities (14:1). Among the religious authorities, the chief priests especially will stand out.[47] All other characters—the disciples and Judas, the crowd, Pilate, the Roman soliders, the women, Joseph of Arimathea, and even the young man in white—are secondary regardless of how necessary or prominent their roles. Primarily, the conflict is between Jesus and the authorities.

Mark narrates that the chief priests and the scribes search how they might arrest and kill Jesus "by deceit" ("cunning") (14:1). With this strong comment, Mark characterizes all the actions of the religious authorities in the passion account as in some sense reflecting the trait of "deceitfulness." Add to this the further comment that the authorities, in doing away with Jesus, want to avoid provoking an uproar among the people (14:2), and earlier notations of Mark rush to mind: Ever since Jesus' first round of clashes with the religious authorities, the latter have been conspiring how to destroy him (3:6; 11:18; 12:12). In the passion account, then, Mark will finally tell of the outcome of the authorities' long-standing conspiracy against Jesus.

After the arrest of Jesus and until his death,[48] Mark once again depicts Jesus as passive, as at the beginning of the story (1:1-13). Until his arrest, however, Jesus demonstrates that he is in full command of events by foretelling them or interpreting their meaning. To present Jesus in this light is of paramount importance to Mark, for he wishes to show that Jesus goes to his death not as a helpless or hapless victim, but as one who, in obedience to the Father, willingly embraces the fate of the cross. Consequently, the irony of Jesus' passion is that if the religious authorities will the death of Jesus, so do God and Jesus, but for opposite reasons: The authorities want Jesus dead because they see in him an ally of Satan who threatens their position and authority and Israel's survival as a people; God and Jesus will the death of Jesus because by it salvation will be accomplished for all.

Illustrations of Jesus' command of events prior to his arrest abound. For example, when the woman pours expensive ointment on his head in the house of Simon the leper, Jesus counters those complaining that this was a waste by interpreting her act as the anointing of his body for burial (14:3-9). So as to celebrate the Passover, Jesus sends two disciples equipped with elaborate instructions to find the room where they are to make preparations, and Mark notes that the disciples found everything just as Jesus told them (14:12-16). During their last supper together and on the way to the Mount of Olives, Jesus makes three predictions concerning the disciples: One of the twelve will betray him; all of them will abandon him; and Peter will deny him (14:17-21, 26-31). Also during the last supper, Jesus interprets for the disciples the significance of his impending death: "This is my blood of the covenant, which is poured out for many" (14:22-25). At Gethsemane, the reader learns from Jesus the proper understanding of his suffering: It is symbolic not, say, of heroic martyrdom but of obedient submission to the Father's will (14:32-41). Also at Gethsemane, Jesus predicts the imminent arrival of his betrayer to arrest him (14:42). And immediately following his arrest, Jesus expresses his keen awareness that, ultimately, it is the hand of God at work in his passion, for these events occur "that the scriptures might be fulfilled" (14:49).

After he is arrested, Jesus silently submits to the will of his captors, Judas and the crowd. They, in turn, hand him over for trial to his arch-adversaries, the chief priests, elders, and scribes, who make up the Sanhedrin (14:53, 55-65). These groups are the very ones to whom Jesus earlier told his parable of the wicked husbandmen. Determined to condemn Jesus to death, they hear from numerous witnesses. The testimony of the witnesses, however, is false and conflicting, so that Jesus continues to remain silent. Finally, however, the high priest himself seizes the initiative. As the presiding officer of the Sanhedrin, he is aware of Jesus' parable of the wicked husbandmen. Shrewdly, he takes the claim Jesus raised in his parable, rephrases it, and hurls it back at Jesus in the form of a question: "Are you the Messiah, the Son of the Blessed [God]?" Suddenly confronted with the truth of his identity, Jesus responds in two ways. He first breaks his silence and resolutely replies, "I am!" Then he directs an ominous word of his own against both the high priest and the Sanhedrin: He will be "the man," he asserts, whom they will soon see sitting at the right hand of God and coming for judgment on the clouds of heaven. At this, the high priest demonstratively declares Jesus to be guilty of blasphemy,[49] and the whole Sanhedrin condemns him to death.

In these scenes of Jesus' trial, the element of irony suffuses Mark's story. In Jesus' case, the irony is that he is condemned to death for committing blasphemy, that is, for infringing upon the majesty of God.[50] Still, the only "crime" of which Jesus is guilty is daring to claim to be the one who God said he is at the baptism and the transfiguration. The upshot is that Jesus is made to die for claiming to be who he is, the Son of God. In the case of the high priest and the Sanhedrin, the irony is that, in condemning Jesus to death for blaspheming God, they in effect allege that they know the mind of God. Alleging to know the mind of God, they unwittingly act contrary to God: They repudiate the notion that Jesus is God's Son and bring about the Son's death. Confronted once again with the truth of Jesus' identity, they reject this truth and demonstrate that they have in no wise penetrated the secret of his identity.

As Jesus foretold in his third passion prediction, the Jewish authorities hand him over to gentiles, to Pilate and the Romans (15:1-27). Before Pilate, the charge brought against Jesus is sedition: Jesus claims to be king (15:1, 26). Consequently, Pilate too is curious about who Jesus says he is. Right off, he asks Jesus whether he is the "King of the Jews" (15:2). In the ears of a Roman like Pilate, to admit to being "King of the Jews" is to admit to being an insurrectionist and false claimant to the throne of Israel (15:26). Because Jesus, though not an insurrectionist, is in fact the King of the Jews, he answers Pilate's question in the affirmative ("So you say"; 15:2). For their part, the chief priests seize on Jesus' answer to accuse him of "many things," that is, acts of sedition (15:3). Because the chief priests' accusations are false, Jesus acquits them all with silence (15:4-5).

The malice the chief priests exhibit at Jesus' hearing convinces Pilate that Jesus is innocent and that they have handed him over out of envy (15:10). Indeed, Pilate himself attests to Jesus' innocence by distancing himself from the very term "King of the Jews." Because to him this term connotes that Jesus is an insurrectionist and he holds this to be a lie, Pilate lets the crowd know that "King of the Jews" is their term for Jesus, not his (15:12). At the same time, Pilate also takes a stab at getting Jesus freed. Cleverly, he believes he can achieve this by making use of his yearly custom of releasing at the Feast of the Passover some prisoner the crowd is pleased to select. Forcing a choice between Jesus and one Barabbas, a murderer and known insurrectionist, Pilate asks the crowd whether it does not desire that Jesus be released (15:6-9). Pilate's ploy, however, fails. Intervening, the chief priests stir the crowd to call for Barabbas's release and Jesus' crucifixion (15:11-14). Anxious to satisfy the crowd, Pilate acquiesces: Barabbas is set free and Jesus is delivered to the soldiers to be crucified (15:15). Undeniably, Jesus has lost the struggle for the hearts of the crowd in which he was engaged throughout his ministry: The crowd has chosen, and it stands at the side of its leaders.

Taking Jesus inside Pilate's residence, the Roman soldiers make coarse mockery of him (15:16-20). The irony is that in so doing, they disclose what it truly means for Jesus to be the "King of the Jews." Clothing Jesus in purple, placing a crown of thorns on his head, and kneeling before him in mock homage, the soldiers strike his head with a reed, spit upon him, and salute him with "Hail, King of the Jews!" Later, the religious authorities will also mock Jesus, addressing him as he hangs on the cross as "the King of Israel" (15:31-32). In Markan perspective, Jesus is indeed the King of the Jews [Israel], yet not as one who aspires to political or military rule but as one who serves and saves his people through suffering.

As he is led to the cross and crucified (15:20b-39), Jesus stands out ever more prominently as the one who, though righteous, nonetheless suffers.[51] Jesus virtually lives out, for example, the afflictions described in Psalm 22 (15:24, 29, 34) and Psalm 69 (15:36). In so doing, however, he also exemplifies perfectly the wholeness that is the hallmark of his relationship to God: He demonstrates that he loves God with heart, soul, mind, and strength.[52] Jesus loves God with all his heart, for out of obedience to God he suffers the pangs of thirst (15:23).[53] Jesus loves God with mind and strength, for out of obedience to God he relinquishes even the last remnant of his earthly possessions, his clothes (15:24).[54] And Jesus loves God with all his soul, for out of obedience to God he resists the temptation to save his life either by descending from the cross (as the passers-by, the religious authorities, and the two insurrectionists challenge him to do) or by calling upon Elijah for deliverance (as those at the foot of the cross mistakenly believe he does) (15:29-32, 35-36). Uttering two great cries, Jesus expires as one perfectly obedient to God who trusts that not even death can frustrate God's will to vindicate him.

With the death of Jesus on the cross, the reader has reached the climax of Mark's story. At the cross, the two great themes concerning Jesus' identity and destiny both intersect and culminate. Seeing Jesus die, the Roman centurion standing opposite him experiences a change of heart and exclaims, "Truly this man was the Son of God!" (15:39). As a character who makes only a brief appearance in Mark's story, the centurion is not the one who need understand the profundity of his words but the reader. For the reader, the centurion's acclamation is climactic.

The centurion asserts that Jesus "truly" was the Son of God. At his trial, the Jewish Sanhedrin abjectly repudiated Jesus' claim to be God's Son. In light of this, the centurion's acclamation becomes a vindication of Jesus' claim: He was indeed the Son of God.

The centurion says that Jesus "was" the Son of God. The past tense "was" is appropriate because the centurion has just witnessed Jesus die. The death of Jesus marks the end of his earthly ministry. The end of Jesus' ministry, however, is, at the same time, its climax. God's immediate response to Jesus' death is to cause the curtain of the temple to be torn in two from top to bottom (15:38). The significance of this act is that it portends the destruction of the temple[55] and therefore also the cessation of the temple cult. By his death, Jesus sheds his blood, establishing a new covenant and atoning for the sins of all humankind, and thus accomplishes salvation.[56] At the last supper,[57] Jesus foretold as much: "This is my blood of the covenant, which is poured out for many" (14:24).

Last, the centurion declares that Jesus was "the Son of God." For the first time in Mark's story, a human character other than Jesus himself (12:6) publicly and unreservedly views Jesus the way God views him. The result is that the centurion becomes the first human to penetrate the secret of Jesus' identity and understand aright who he is. At the cross, Jesus' identity is fully unveiled even as his destiny has become fully known. From here the reader can look back over the whole of Mark's story. He or she can see that Jesus is the Son of God not only as one who authoritatively preaches, calls disciples, teaches, heals, and exorcises demons (1:14—8:26) but also, and especially, as one who journeys to Jerusalem and, in perfect obedience to God, suffers and dies for the sins of all (8:27—16:8). Destiny illuminates identity and identity destiny as the secret of Jesus' identity comes to light.

If Mark's story reaches its culmination in the cross, it concludes with the resurrection (16:1-8). The message the young man in white gives the women is that Jesus of Nazareth, who remains the crucified one, has been raised by God and will go before his disciples to Galilee, where they will see him (16:6-7). By describing Jesus as "the one who has been, and remains, the crucified," the young man says in effect that the risen Jesus is one with the crucified Jesus.[58] Just as the crucified Jesus was God's beloved Son, so the risen Jesus, who still bears on his person the marks of crucifixion, is God's beloved Son.

The young man stresses that Jesus has been raised by God (16:6). In Jesus' death and resurrection, the conflict between him and Israel comes to fundamental, though not final, resolution. As the religious authorities condemned Jesus to death, they were confident they acted with God's approval: Israel was to be purged of an agent of Satan so that people, law, tradition, temple, and they themselves as Israel's chosen leaders might be preserved. Moreover, in witnessing Jesus die on the cross, the authorities believed they accomplished their objective. Ironically, however, God shows, by raising Jesus from the dead, that Jesus is the one vindicated: In his conflict with Israel, God puts Jesus in the right. What this means most immediately for the authorities is that because they repudiated God's Son, they will, just as Jesus predicted, suffer punishment and forfeit their position of authority (12:9). Beyond that, it also means that at the end of the age they will see Jesus, the risen and vindicated Son of God, return in power and glory as "the man" God has chosen to usher in his consummated rule.[59] At that time, Jesus' enemies will encounter him as Judge and his followers as deliverer.[60] This future appearance of Jesus constitutes the final resolution of his conflict with Israel and will prove fateful for the nations as well (13:10; 14:9).

Finally, the young man in white also tells the women that the risen Jesus goes before his disciples to Galilee, where they will see him (16:7). Because Mark describes no Galilean meeting between Jesus and the disciples, neither does he recount how Jesus' conflict with the disciples over the meaning of true discipleship is ultimately resolved. Instead, Mark leaves it to the reader to project the resolution of this conflict. Precisely what shape this resolution takes is a matter we shall discuss in chapter 4.

Summary

Mark's story of Jesus is a story of conflict between Jesus and Israel, made up of the crowd and the religious authorities. In the beginning of the story (1:1-13), Mark presents Jesus to the reader by telling first of John the Baptist and then of Jesus. Both John and Jesus stand forth as agents of God sent by God. John, however, is the forerunner of Jesus, who readies Israel for Jesus' coming and reflects in his person and fate the person and fate of Jesus. The high point of the beginning follows the baptism of Jesus. God himself enters the world of the story, empowering Jesus for messianic ministry and declaring that he, the Messiah-King from the line of David, is his royal Son. Since this is God's understanding of Jesus, it is normative for Mark's story. In the temptation, Jesus Son of God shows why God sent him: To bind the strong man Satan and inaugurate the end-time age of salvation.

In the middle of the story (1:14—8:26), Mark describes Jesus' public ministry in Israel. As the one in whom God in his end-time rule draws near to humankind, Jesus summons Israel to repentance and to belief in the gospel he proclaims. Traversing the whole of Galilee, Jesus preaches, calls disciples, teaches, heals, and exorcises demons. His fame goes forth, and while the crowd throngs to him and is well disposed toward him, the religious leaders utterly oppose him, even plotting his death. At the same time, while supernatural beings such as demons know Jesus' identity as God's Son, human beings do not. Instead, they wonder and speculate about who he might be, with the Jewish public deciding he is some sort of prophet.

In the lengthy end section of his story (8:27—16:8), Mark tells of Jesus' journey to Jerusalem, of his stay in the temple, and of his suffering, death, and rising. Mark interweaves the themes of Jesus' identity and destiny: Not until Jesus' destiny is fully known is his identity as God's Son finally affirmed by a human other than himself.

To focus on Jesus' identity, Mark progressively unveils it in three stages. In the first stage, Peter confesses on behalf of the disciples that Jesus is the Messiah. This confession is correct but insufficient: It is correct because it views Jesus as God's Anointed sent to preach, teach, heal, and exorcise demons. It is insufficient because it does not envisage suffering and death for Jesus. In the second stage, Jesus is recognized as the Son of David. This confession too is correct but insufficient: It is correct because Jesus stands in the line of David. It is insufficient because Jesus is the Son of God and therefore "more" than the Son of David. In the third stage, the centurion at the cross affirms Jesus to be the Son of God. For the first time in Mark's story, a human other than Jesus correctly and sufficiently "thinks" about Jesus the way God "thinks" about him.

To turn to Jesus' destiny, the cross is also the place where the reader can look back over Jesus' ministry and understand his mission. God sent Jesus not only to preach, call disciples, teach, heal, and exorcise demons but also to suffer and die (and rise). Sent by God to suffer and die, both God and Jesus will Jesus' death, for by it he establishes a new covenant and accomplishes atonement for sins and universal salvation. Ironically, the religious authorities (and, in the passion, all Israel) also will the death of Jesus. They look upon Jesus as an ally of Satan and a threat to people, tradition, law, temple, and their own authority as Israel's leaders.

The death and resurrection of Jesus become the place where Mark's story reaches its climax and comes to fundamental, though not final, resolution. Believing that they are doing God's will, the religious authorities bring about the death of Jesus. In their perspective, they have successfully purged Israel of him. God, however, raises Jesus from the dead. He thus vindicates him and shows that, ironically, he was the one who was in the right in his conflict with Israel.

In the immediate future, Jesus' vindication will mean the punishment and downfall of the authorities. At the end of the age, however, it will also mean that Jesus, the risen and vindicated Son of God, will return as "the man" God has chosen to usher in his consummated rule. At that time, he will judge his enemies and deliver his followers. It is Jesus' return at the end of the age, therefore, that Mark regards as the final resolution of his story of Jesus.

EXCURSUS: Jesus' Use of "the Son of Man"

In the course of Mark's story, Jesus not infrequently refers to himself as "the Son of man."[61] Because of the special way in which this term is used, a word on it is in order here.[62]

As a designation for Jesus, "the Son of man" stands in a category by itself. It is distinctive because it is both "like" and "unlike" the major christological titles of Mark's story. The major titles are "Messiah," "the King of the Jews [Israel]," "the Son of David," and "the Son of God."

Like the major titles, "the Son of man" applies to Jesus in a way in which it can be applied to no other human being. Thus, because it occurs exclusively in Jesus' mouth as a self-designation, it refers to no one but him. Second, it reflects the three principal phases of Jesus' unique ministry: his present activity on earth (e.g., 2:10, 28); his suffering, death, and rising (e.g., 8:31); and his anticipated Parousia (e.g., 13:26). And third, it also depicts Jesus, in certain of his sayings, as fulfilling OT prophecy (e.g., 13:26; 14:21, 62).

Unlike the major titles, "the Son of man" is never used to apprise the reader or other characters within Mark's story of the identity of Jesus, of "who he is." If one glances at the major titles, one finds numerous statements or questions such as these: "You are the Messiah!" (8:29); "Are you the King of the Jews?" (15:2); "The scribes say that the Messiah is the Son of David" (12:35); "You are the Son of God!" (3:11); and "Are you the Messiah, the Son of the Blessed?" (14:61). What one does not find in Mark, however, is statements or questions

parallel to these featuring "the Son of man." Never does anyone say or ask: "You are (Are you?) the Son of man"; or "He
is (Is he?) the Son of man."

To see how striking this phenomenon is, consider how characters systematically ignore "the Son of man" when construing
the identity of Jesus. Supernatural beings such as God and
demons know the identity of Jesus, yet they never call him
"the Son of man" but "the Son of God" (e.g., 1:11; 3:11; 9:7).
Though the disciples have heard Jesus designate himself as
"the Son of man" (2:23-28), when Peter confesses him on
behalf of all, he terms him "the Messiah!" (8:29). Similarly,
though the crowd, or Jewish public, too, has heard Jesus refer
to himself as "the Son of man" (2:1-12),[63] it conceives of him
not as "the Son of man" but as a prophet (6:14-16; 8:28).
And though Jesus has also referred to himself as "the Son of
man" in the presence of some scribes and the Pharisees (2:1-
12, 23-28), the high priest at Jesus' trial does not ask him
whether he is "the Son of man" but whether he is "the Messiah,
the Son of the Blessed [God]" (14:61). In Mark's story, "the
Son of man" is used by neither supernatural beings nor human beings to ask or declare "who Jesus is."

Do Jesus' Parousia sayings constitute an exception to the
rule that "the Son of man" does not set forth his identity? Or
to put the question differently, is the Jesus who comes at the
end of the age to be identified as "the Son of man" (8:38;
13:26; 14:62)? The evidence indicates otherwise. In 8:38,
Jesus tacitly refers to himself in the hearing not just of the
disciples but also of the crowd (8:34) as "the Son of man"
who will come in the glory of his Father with the holy angels
to usher in God's splendid kingdom. Yet this reference of
Jesus to himself as "the Son of man," which is both public
and eschatological in the strictest sense, stirs no one—neither
the crowd nor the disciples nor, later, the high priest at Jesus'
trial (14:61) nor the religious leaders beneath the cross (15:31-
32)—to construe "the Son of man" as setting forth Jesus'
identity. In Mark's story, the Jesus who will one day come in
the glory of "his Father" is, in identity, "the Son of God" (1:1,
11; 9:7; 13:32).

As to meaning, the Greek term underlying "the Son of man" may be translated as "the man," or "the human being." It cannot be reduced simply to the equivalent of the pronoun "I" ("me") or "a man," because it is consistently definite in form (" 'the' Son of man"). Still, to substitute "the man" or "the human being" each time "the Son of man" appears is to incur a problem. The problem is that in so doing, one does not always make it as clear as it must be that "the Son of man" refers explicitly to Jesus. One can observe in Jesus' saying in 2:27-28 the ambiguity that can arise: "The sabbath was made for man, not man for the sabbath; so 'the man' [any man? any human being?] is lord even of the sabbath" (also 2:10). To preclude such ambiguity, I suggest that "the Son of man" be rendered in English as "this man," or "this human being." The expression "this man," or "this human being," is what may be called a translational equivalent. The strength of substituting "this man" or "this human being" for "the Son of man" is that it makes it unmistakably clear that "the Son of man" always refers to Jesus: "The sabbath was made for man, not man for the sabbath; so 'this man' is lord even of the sabbath" (2:27-28); " 'This man' will be delivered into the hands of men, and they will kill him" (9:31); "I am, and you will see 'this man' sitting at the right hand of power and coming with the clouds of heaven" (14:62).

If "the Son of man" means "the man," or "the human being" (and "this man," or "this human being," can serve as its translational equivalent), one can readily understand how Jesus can frequently refer to himself openly or in public as "the Son of man" and yet no one, neither supernatural being nor human being, will ever ask him whether he is "the Son of man" or declare him to be such. In Mark's story "the Son of man" is, again, not used to convey to either reader or characters the identity of Jesus. The Jesus who refers to himself as "the Son of man" is the Messiah-King from the line of David, the royal Son of God.

In Mark's story, then, "the Son of man" is best understood not as a christological title but as a technical term. The very purpose of a christological title is to set forth, wholly or partially, both the identity and the significance of Jesus. By contrast, a technical term is, less grandly, some word or expression bearing a precise meaning. Whereas "the Son of man" does bear a precise meaning ("the man," or "the human being") and also can be said to convey something of the significance of Jesus, it does not set forth his identity.

This leaves a final question: What purpose does "the Son of man" serve in Mark's story? In designating himself as "the Son of man," Jesus points to himself as the man who, though acting on divine authority (2:10, 28), is repudiated by Israel and gentiles (10:33-34) but vindicated by God (now in the resurrection; later at his Parousia [14:62]). In Mark's story, therefore, the designation "the Son of man" emphasizes the twin features of repudiation and vindication.

3
The Story of the
AUTHORITIES

Mark's story is one of conflict, and conflict is the force that propels the story forward. The major conflict is between Jesus and Israel, made up of the religious authorities and the Jewish crowd. Since the crowd does not turn against Jesus until his arrest, his antagonists are the authorities. Except for the "friendly scribe," they are the ones who invariably "think the things not of God, but of humans." Their story is the one we shall trace in this chapter.

The groups comprising the religious authorities are the Pharisees, the Sadducees, the Herodians, the chief priests, the scribes, and the elders.[1] Apart from the Herodians, all are well known in Jewish history.[2] In Jesus' own day, the Pharisees and the Sadducees stood in stark contrast to each other. The Pharisees were progressive, a party among, though not of, the people.[3] Their goal was that Israel should become the righteous nation of the covenant. To this end they taught compliance with the "tradition of the elders," an oral code of conduct effectively adapting the law of Moses to later times and changing demands.[4] By contrast, the Sadducees were a wealthy, conservative party concentrated in Jerusalem. Their members were from aristocratic families of patrician and priestly stock. They refused adherence to the tradition of the elders and advocated a rigorous application of the law of Moses to the life of the nation. In general, they espoused a political and religious policy, including cooperation with Rome, aimed at preserving the status quo.

The factor distinguishing the chief priests, scribes, and elders was the office they held or the profession they practiced. The chief priests occupied a hereditary office by virtue of which they supervised the temple in Jerusalem and the sacrificial system. Scribes were the theologians and lawyers of the time, expert at interpreting the law governing Jewish society. This law was that of Moses and, for the Pharisees, the oral tradition as well.[5] And the elders were men of wealth and the leaders of aristocratic families. Along with the more influential chief priests and scribes, they served on the Sanhedrin, or High Council.[6] Presided over by the high priest, the Sanhedrin numbered seventy-one members. It functioned as the domestic government of Judea,[7] conducting its business in a hall located on the grounds of the temple. Although ultimately subject to the authority of the Roman prefect (who in Mark's story is Pilate), the Sanhedrin exercised broad powers of a religious, judicial, and financial nature.

In addition to these groups, Mark also makes mention of the Herodians. Historically, it is difficult to be certain who they were.[8] In Mark's own presentation, they function in effect as "religious authorities" because of their close association with the Pharisees (3:6; 12:13). At the same time, it appears they are also to be thought of as agents of Herod Antipas (8:15), the petty king and son of Herod the Great. Antipas, ruler of Galilee and Perea, is the one who orders the beheading of John the Baptist (6:14-29). Since John is the forerunner of Jesus, Antipas poses a threat also to Jesus and the disciples. Jesus, in fact, warns the disciples to be on their guard against the evil influence of Antipas (8:15).

In the way Mark deals with the religious authorities in his story, the peculiarities of each group are only marginally apparent. The scribes, who seem to be thought of as Pharisaic by persuasion (2:16), are the most prominent of Jesus' opponents. Except in the passion narrative itself (chaps. 14–16), the Pharisees, too, frequently confront him. However, once Jesus enters Jerusalem and the temple, his main opponents become the authorities making up the Sanhedrin. The chief priests, joined by the scribes, lead the opposition[9] and are at times abetted by the elders. The chief priests are the ones, for example, with whom Judas strikes his deal (14:10-11). Despite these nuances, what characterizes the authorities most is that they form a united front in the relentless opposition they all mount against Jesus. For this reason, they can be treated as a single character.

Conflict over Authority

Mark does not introduce the reader to the religious authorities until the middle of his story (1:14—8:26). The reason is apparent: The reader must first acquire a firm understanding of Jesus. Accordingly, Mark uses the beginning of his story (1:1-13) to present Jesus to the reader. Also, in the middle of his story he describes Jesus as embarking on his public ministry to Israel. In preaching, Jesus announces that because a new time has dawned and God in his rule has drawn near, Israel is to reorder its life and trust in the message he proclaims. In calling disciples, Jesus forms a circle of twelve, the nucleus of an end-time Israel. In teaching, Jesus declares the will of God and challenges Pharisaic teaching concerning law and tradition. And in healing and exorcising demons, Jesus tacitly claims it is in him that God is at work to overthrow the kingdom of Satan.

In their perspective, the religious authorities believe they are the ones God has appointed to be the rulers and guardians of his chosen people Israel. Because they are God's agents, their teaching concerning law and tradition is both authoritative and normative. To oppose them is to oppose God, and to challenge their rule and teaching is to summon Israel to stray from God's rule and teaching. In their eyes, therefore, Jesus poses the gravest sort of threat. Not only does he call the legitimacy of their leadership into question but he is also a menace to the spiritual well-being of Israel as a whole. Given the authorities' views concerning Jesus, one can surmise that conflict between them and Jesus is inevitable. The only question is when it will occur and how it will develop.

Authority as the Critical Issue of the Conflict

Mark raises the specter of conflict in the first summary-passage devoted to the teaching of Jesus (1:21-22). He reports that Jesus enters the synagogue of Capernaum on the sabbath and teaches. Noting that the people react to Jesus with astonishment, Mark explains: "For he was teaching them as one who has authority, and not as the scribes." This comment reflects Mark's own positive assessment of Jesus and negative assessment of the religious authorities (in the persons of the scribes). It invites the reader to look with disfavor upon the authorities and to anticipate conflict between Jesus and them.[10]

That Mark should allude to impending conflict in a summary-passage highlighting teaching is not mere happenstance. Of all that Jesus does during his public ministry to Israel, teaching is what is "customary" of him (10:1). As if to underscore this, Mark depicts disciples, strangers, and opponents alike as addressing Jesus as "teacher," or "rabbi."[11] While "teacher" is not a title of majesty, it is nonetheless an honored term of human respect. By the same token, if one takes Jesus' controversies with the religious authorities into account, teaching can likewise be said to constitute the principal activity Mark attributes to them. Consequently, for Mark to give a first hint of conflict in a passage emphasizing teaching is for him to associate conflict with the activity most typical of the ministries of both Jesus and the authorities. This explains why his comment that Jesus, unlike the authorities (scribes), engages in teaching as one endowed with divine authority captures the reader's attention.

Overall, the extreme importance of Mark's comment is that it identifies "authority" as the critical issue around which Jesus' conflict with the religious authorities will revolve. Moreover, it also advises the reader that the controversies Jesus will have with the authorities are all to be decided in favor of Jesus.

Jesus will always be right, for he will "think the things of God." The authorities will always be wrong, for they will "think the things of humans." The upshot is that Jesus will prove himself to be Israel's true shepherd, the royal Son whom God has sent to teach the leaderless people (6:34). Conversely, the authorities will prove themselves to be both evildoers (3:4, 6) and hypocrites (7:6-7): hypocrites, because in professing to teach the will of God, they will teach instead doctrines of their own devising; and evildoers, because in the mistaken belief that they know God's will, they will bring about the death of his Son.

The Intensification of the Conflict

Fundamentally, therefore, Mark presents Jesus' conflict with the religious authorities as one of authority: Does Jesus or does he not discharge his ministry as one authorized by God? As this conflict unfolds, it becomes progressively more intense, until it finally ends in Jesus' death. Here in the middle of Mark's story (1:14—8:26), three factors in particular contribute to this progressive intensification of the conflict: (*a*) the comment Mark makes after only the first cycle of controversies that the Pharisees and the Herodians go off and consult on how to destroy Jesus (3:6); (*b*) the overall trend[12] in the controversies from indirect confrontation with Jesus or the disciples to direct confrontation with Jesus whereby Jesus is himself challenged to defend his own actions; and (*c*) the parallel trend in the controversies according to which the emphasis shifts from questions having to do with blasphemy, tradition, and Mosaic law to the question about authority itself.

To examine these factors, the most obvious way Mark heightens the intensity of Jesus' conflict with the religious authorities is through the comment he makes that the Pharisees, joined by the Herodians, withdraw to deliberate on how to destroy Jesus (3:6). This comment, which comes early in the middle of the story, is of dual significance. For one thing, it characterizes the authorities in the persons of the Pharisees as evildoers who are hard of heart (3:4-5). Whereas Jesus uses the sabbath to do good and to save by healing, the authorities use the sabbath to do evil and to begin plotting how to kill Jesus (3:4, 6). For another thing, Mark's comment also dispels any false illusions the reader may still have about the utter seriousness of Jesus' conflict with the authorities: From early on, this conflict is to the death.

The second way Mark heightens the intensity of the conflict between Jesus and the religious authorities has to do with the way he structures and arranges Jesus' controversies. In general, Mark so structures and arranges them that the trend is from indirect confrontation with Jesus or the disciples to direct confrontation with Jesus. The culmination of this trend comes in Jesus' final clash with the authorities in the middle of the story (8:11-13): In demanding of Jesus a sign from heaven, the Pharisees at last challenge him directly on a matter pertaining strictly to him. In terms of the whole of Mark's story, this means that at the time the authorities first retire to hatch a conspiracy against Jesus (3:6), they do so without so much as having confronted him openly for something he himself has said or done.

This trend from indirect to direct confrontation in the middle of Mark's story can be readily traced. Thus, some of the scribes, in charging Jesus with blasphemy because he has forgiven the paralytic his sins, utter their charge, not aloud, but only "in their hearts" (2:1-12). The scribes of the Pharisees, in taking umbrage at Jesus for eating with toll collectors and sinners, do not approach Jesus himself but the disciples (2:15-17). Certain people, disturbed because Jesus' disciples break custom and do not fast, approach Jesus but with a question about the disciples (2:18-20). The Pharisees, in demanding to know why Jesus' disciples have broken the sabbath law by working, likewise approach Jesus, but, again, about the disciples (2:23-28). These same Pharisees, having closely watched Jesus so as to have reason to condemn him for unlawfully healing on the sabbath, remain silent when openly confronted by him and refuse to state their accusation against him (3:1-6). The scribes from Jerusalem, in asserting that

Jesus exorcises demons on the authority of the prince of demons, slander him but not to his face (3:22-30). The Pharisees and some of the scribes, in observing the disciples violate the tradition of the elders by eating with unwashed hands, approach Jesus, but, once again, about the disciples (7:1-13). Finally, the Pharisees, in demanding that Jesus give them a sign from heaven, at last do what their confederates have not previously dared to do: challenge Jesus directly on a matter relating to his own actions (8:11-13). At this, Mark has so guided events in the middle of his story that the conflict between Jesus and the authorities has intensified to the point where it has become acutely confrontational: Attacks are no more indirect but face-to-face.

The third way Mark heightens the intensity of the conflict between Jesus and the religious authorities is through a notable shift in the kind of issues being debated: The trend is from matters dealing implicitly with the issue of authority to matters dealing explicitly with this issue. To trace this trend, the first matter sparking debate centers on the charge that Jesus commits blasphemy against God (2:7). This charge, however, is exceptional in the sense that it is also the charge for which the Sanhedrin finally condemns Jesus to death (14:64). In Mark's story, then, the first charge the authorities make against Jesus foreshadows the climactic charge they make against him.

Following this charge, one observes a progression in the subject matter being disputed. First, it is the tradition of the elders (2:15-17, 18-20). Next, it is Mosaic law (2:23-28; 3:1-5). Last, it is the topic of authority itself, as treated in an alternating pattern: (*a*) The authorities charge Jesus with deriving his authority from the prince of demons (3:22-30); (*b*) Jesus charges the authorities with using their authority to cultivate tradition at the expense of obeying the word of God (7:1-13); and (*c*) the authorities challenge Jesus to prove by a sign from heaven that God is in truth the source of his authority (8:11-13). Finally, in a private comment Jesus warns the disciples to be on the alert against the evil intentions[13] of both the authorities (Pharisees) and Herod (8:15).

The Course of the Conflict

Thus far, we have observed that at the center of Jesus' conflict with the religious authorities is the issue of "authority" and that, as this conflict develops, it becomes progressively more intense. Now we need to sketch the conflict itself.

The First Cycle of Controversies.   Throughout the middle of Mark's story (1:14—8:26), Jesus' clashes with the religious authorities are intermittent but fierce. The first clashes, which occur early in Jesus' ministry, constitute a cycle of five controversies and end on the note that the Pharisees are incited by Jesus to conspire to destroy him (2:1—3:6).[14]

To explore this cycle, Jesus himself triggers the first controversy (2:1-12). When a paralytic is brought to him for healing, Jesus forgives the man his sins. Since in Mark's world sickness can be viewed as symptomatic of sin,[15] granting forgiveness can become a means for accomplishing healing. Witnessing Jesus forgive the man, some of the scribes sitting there consider "in their hearts" that he has made himself guilty of blasphemy. By announcing forgiveness, Jesus has arrogated to himself the authority of God and therefore infringed on the majesty of God.[16] To demonstrate that he does in fact possess the authority to forgive sins, Jesus utters a second word, instantly healing the paralytic. Whereas this awesome display of authority quiets the scribes, all the people are amazed and glorify God.

The second controversy too is touched off by Jesus (2:15-17). Observing him recline at table with many toll collectors and sinners, the scribes of the Pharisees quickly voice objection. Specifically, Jesus is in violation of the tradition of the elders. As this tradition dictates, meals are to be eaten in a state of ritual purity.[17] When so eaten, they provide an opportunity to extend to the sphere of everyday life the purity characteristic of priests in the temple.[18] Hence, at mealtime one finds oneself in the presence of God. By contrast, to eat with toll collectors and sinners is to make oneself ritually impure. Toll collectors have dealings with gentiles and are regarded as no better than thieves and robbers.[19] Sinners live in disregard of God's law or pursue dishonorable vocations.[20] By inviting such disreputable persons as toll collectors and sinners to have table fellowship with him, Jesus grants them forgiveness and invites them to live in the sphere of God's gracious rule.[21] Offended at what they see, the scribes of the Pharisees approach not Jesus but the disciples and demand to know why Jesus behaves as he does. Overhearing their question, Jesus retorts that the very purpose of his ministry is to summon, not "righteous" such as they, but sinners.

In the third controversy, not Jesus but the disciples precipitate conflict (2:18-22). Unlike the disciples of both John and the Pharisees, Jesus' disciples do not fast. Failure to fast, however, constitutes a serious breach of custom. In the eyes of first-century Pharisees, it placed one at odds with the tradition of the elders. Fasting symbolized contrition for sin and ranked as one of the cardinal virtues of their piety. For this reason, Pharisees fasted on both Mondays and Thursdays.[22] Aroused because Jesus' disciples do not fast, people come to him wanting an explanation. Jesus, however, turns them away, comparing the disciples to guests at a wedding (or to grooms-men) and himself to the bridegroom. Jesus' point is that the present is a time of joy and celebration, as at a wedding, not a time of sorrow and mourning. Once the bridegroom shall have been "taken away" from the guests, then the time for fasting will have come. Through the use of this imagery, Jesus cryptically refers to himself as the Messiah Son of God, to his ministry as the time of the gospel and salvation, and to his departure as the time of his death. Although the reader understands the imagery, it is lost on the characters within Mark's story.

In the fourth controversy, the disciples once again incite conflict (2:23-28). While walking on a path through fields of grain, they pluck heads of wheat. Spotting them, the Pharisees come up to Jesus and query him on why the disciples are doing what is unlawful on the sabbath. At issue here is not violation of tradition but of Mosaic law. The Pharisees adjudge that by plucking grain, the disciples are unlawfully reaping on the sabbath and hence not observing God's command to rest (Exod. 20:8-11; Deut. 5:12-15). In defense of the disciples, Jesus gives two replies. In the first (2:25-26), he scores his point by arguing from an example in scripture (1 Sam. 21:1-6). In the case of David and his men, scripture itself shows that, under exceptional circumstances, human need might rightly be regarded as taking precedence over the law.[23] In his second reply (2:27-28), Jesus scores two further points. In principle, the law was created by God for the sake of humans and not humans for the sake of the law. Consequently, he, "the man" who has authority over the sabbath, is fully authorized to permit his needy disciples to pluck grain on the sabbath.

Finally, in the last controversy Jesus again becomes the one provoking conflict (3:1-5). Entering the synagogue of Capernaum on the sabbath, he is watched closely by the Pharisees. A man with a withered hand is there, and the Pharisees want to see whether Jesus will heal him. By their rules, to heal this man on the sabbath is to break the law, for the man is in no danger of dying and could be healed on another day. Like the previous controversy, therefore, this one too concerns not tradition but Mosaic law. Turning to the Pharisees, Jesus challenges their interpretation of the law. Through the rhetorical question he poses, he insists that it is always lawful on the sabbath to do good and to save life. Having thus exposed the Pharisees' understanding of the law as narrow and loveless, Jesus heals the man. Without uttering so much as a word, the Pharisees, joined by the Herodians, go away and conspire how to destroy Jesus (3:6). Consequently, by the end of this first cycle of controversies Mark shows that the conflict between Jesus and the religious authorities is already to the death.

The Question of Authority Itself.   Apart from the initial charge of blasphemy, the questions sparking conflict between Jesus and the religious authorities thus far have been tradition and Mosaic law. Although the attacks of the authorities against Jesus have all been indirect and they have still not opposed him to his face for something he himself has done, the conflict between him and them has nonetheless become mortal. As one shifts to the remaining three controversies in the middle of Mark's story, the dispute in each case focuses on the question of authority itself. Also, the pattern according to which this question is dealt with is an alternating one: At issue is (*a*) Jesus' authority, (*b*) their authority, and (*c*) Jesus' authority.

In the first of these controversies, the attack is against Jesus' authority (3:22-30). Thus, scribes, coming to Galilee from Jerusalem, declare either among themselves or to the public that Jesus is able to cast out demons only because he derives his authority from Beelzebul, the prince of demons. In harsh words, Jesus both refutes this allegation and delivers a sharp warning to the scribes. If Beelzebul were the source of his mastery of demons, his exorcisms would be a sign that Satan is at war with himself, which is absurd. Just the opposite, his exorcisms are a sign that he has bound the strong man Satan and is plundering his house by releasing people from his power. In point of fact, the scribes must beware: To attribute to Beelzebul and not God exorcisms performed by divine authority is to slander the Holy Spirit. To slander the Spirit, however, is to make oneself guilty of the one sin God will not pardon.

In the next controversy, Jesus repels an attack against the disciples by himself charging that the religious authorities derive their authority from no source higher than themselves; Jesus' contention, in effect, is that the authorities "think the things not of God, but of humans." Thus, the Pharisees and some of the scribes from Jerusalem, seeing the disciples eat with unwashed hands, approach Jesus demanding to know why the disciples behave in willful disregard of the tradition of the elders (7:1-13). What prompts their question, as Mark explains to the reader, is their concern for ritual purity: The Pharisees and the scribes (indeed, says Mark, "all the Jews," 7:3) eat their meals in a state of ritual purity indicative of the priests in the temple. To eat with unwashed hands, then, does not envisage dirty hands but defiled hands.

In reply to this attack on the disciples, Jesus levels a countercharge (7:6-8) reinforced by an example (7:9-13). Castigating the Pharisees and the scribes as hypocrites, Jesus quotes the prophecy of Isa. 29:13 against them.[24] He assails them for using the observance of tradition as a pretext for abandoning God's will as expressed in Mosaic law. As proof of this accusation, Jesus cites the abuse of the vow of "corban." Through Moses, God has enjoined children to honor father and mother (Exod. 20:12; 21:17). This means children are obligated to care financially for needy parents. But this notwithstanding, should anyone desire to evade this obligation, the Pharisees and the scribes will allow that person to take the vow of corban: One can declare the money that should properly go to one's parents as a gift or offering dedicated to God. The result is that one retains this money for one's own use. In condemning this practice, Jesus denounces it as using tradition to annul the intention of God. Still, the larger charge that Jesus lodges against the Pharisees and the scribes is, again, that the authority they claim they have from God is in reality the product of their own devising.

In Jesus' final and climactic controversy with the religious authorities in the middle of Mark's story, his own authority once more becomes the subject of dispute (8:11-13). Searching Jesus out, the Pharisees demand of him a sign from heaven. With this, the conflict between Jesus and the authorities at last becomes acutely confrontational: For the first time, the authorities challenge Jesus himself on a matter having to do specifically with him. The aim of the Pharisees is to put Jesus to the test concerning the source of his authority. They want him to predict a sign that God will subsequently cause to occur, thus proving incontrovertibly that God stands behind Jesus' ministry.[25] Groaning within himself, Jesus categorically rejects the Pharisees' demand. No sign, he vows, will be given "this generation." Mark's final word on the religious authorities in the middle of his story comes from the mouth of Jesus. Taking leave of the Pharisees who demanded that he prove the source of his authority, Jesus sets sail with his disciples for the other side of the lake. With an eye to the Pharisees, Jesus urgently warns the disciples that they too must be on their guard against the evil intentions of the Pharisees and Herod (8:15).

By the end of the middle of his story (1:14—8:26), Mark leaves the reader in no doubt about both the nature of Jesus' conflict with the religious authorities and the course it will take. Clearly, the critical issue underlying this conflict is that of authority. The religious authorities, whom Mark tells the reader are without authority (1:22), nonetheless believe that they are the chosen agents of God appointed to rule Israel. They therefore view Jesus, not as the supreme agent of God, but as the agent of Satan. Confronted with manifestations of his authority, they accuse him of blasphemy (the charge for which they also condemn him to death) and attack him, though indirectly, on matters of tradition, Mosaic law, and the question of authority itself. Indeed, without ever having challenged Jesus directly for anything he himself has said or done, they even plot to destroy him (3:6). Gradually, however, the conflict between Jesus and the authorities intensifies until at last it does become acutely confrontational: In requesting a sign from heaven, the authorities face Jesus directly concerning a matter pertaining specifically to him (8:11-13). Since at the end of the middle of Mark's story the conflict between Jesus and the authorities is both mortal and acutely confrontational, the reader knows that a conflict this intense will inevitably find its resolution in death.

Conflict in the Temple and Death

In the lengthy end section of his story (8:27—16:8), Mark describes Jesus' journey to Jerusalem and his suffering, death, and rising. To show that Jesus is in command of his fate and to hold before the reader the goal of his story, Mark punctuates the narrative with three passion predictions that Jesus delivers to the disciples (8:31; 9:31; 10:33-34).

"On the way" to Jerusalem, Jesus teaches the disciples and is virtually unencumbered by conflict with the religious authorities. In fact, only twice does he come into contact with them, and once incidentally. After descending from the mount of transfiguration with Peter and the two sons of Zebedee, Jesus finds the other disciples surrounded by a crowd and engaged by the scribes in argument (9:14). The moment Jesus arrives, the scribes fade from view and the crowd, amazed, runs up to Jesus and greets him (9:15). This brief appearance by the scribes serves an obvious purpose: By taking the disciples to task over their inability to heal a demon-possessed boy, the scribes provide opportunity for Jesus to teach the disciples about the power of faith and prayer (9:23, 29).

Later, after Jesus has crossed into the regions beyond the Jordan, the Pharisees confront him so as to put him to the test on the question of divorce (10:2-12). In refutation of their argument that Moses permits divorce (Deut. 24:1), Jesus appeals to the original intention of God, which forbids all divorce. While Jesus' answer silences the Pharisees, it provokes the disciples to ask him about divorce (10:10-12). In different words, Jesus repeats his answer: Divorce is forbidden, for to divorce and remarry is to commit adultery. From this sequence of scenes, it is clear that the primary function of Jesus' debate with the Pharisees is, again, to serve as instruction for the disciples.

Not until Jesus enters Jerusalem, therefore, does sustained conflict occur between him and the religious authorities. The temple becomes the site of conflict leading to the passion, and the passion, in turn, contains within it the fundamental resolution of Jesus' conflict with the authorities.

Further Intensification of the Conflict

If Jesus' conflict with the religious authorities is intense in the middle of Mark's story, it becomes still more intense in the controversies he has with them in the temple (11:27—12:34). To alert the reader to this, Mark makes use of various devices. For one thing, the setting itself heightens the intensity of the conflict, for the temple is the place of God's presence and the seat of the authorities' power. For another thing, the atmosphere in which Jesus' controversies in the temple take place is, except for his exchange with the "friendly scribe," one of unmitigated hostility: Repeatedly, the authorities want to seize Jesus or destroy him (11:18; 12:12). Again, these controversies are also acutely confrontational in tone: In each instance, Jesus is himself challenged by the authorities on matters pertaining specifically to him. Fourth, the questions being contested are all critical in nature, for they have to do, directly or indirectly, with the matter of authority: the authority by which Jesus cleanses the temple (11:15-18, 28), carries out his ministry (11:27-33), or, to the embarrassment of the authorities, sovereignly interprets Mosaic law (12:13-17, 18-27, 28-34). Fifth, uninterruptedly during a single day, all the groups that together make up the united front of the religious authorities approach Jesus so as to oppose him or to get the best of him in debate: the chief priests and the scribes and the elders (11:27), some of the Pharisees and Herodians (12:13), and the Sadducees (12:18). And last, the authorities, unable to defeat Jesus in debate and daring no longer to put any more questions to him (12:34c), finally resort to the one option they believe is still open to them: They withdraw from the temple to search actively for a way to have him arrested and killed (14:1-2). To repeat, through the use of various means Mark deftly calls attention to the heightened intensity of Jesus' conflict with the authorities in the temple.

Conflict in the Temple

Through his astonishing act of cleansing the temple, Jesus himself provokes the intense conflict with the religious authorities that characterizes his stay in the temple and issues in his passion. As Jesus enters Jerusalem, he goes directly to the temple, looks around, and withdraws to Bethany for the night (11:11). Returning from Bethany the next day, he curses a barren fig tree that subsequently withers and dies (11:14, 21). This is symbolic of the fact that although Jesus cleanses the temple, it too is barren of true worship and will one day be destroyed (13:1-3).

After cursing the fig tree, Jesus enters the temple and the court of the gentiles (11:15-19). There he drives out the sellers and buyers, overturns the tables of the money-changers and the seats of those selling doves, allows no one to carry anything through the area, and declares that God's house, which has been turned into a den of robbers, is meant to be a house of prayer for all the nations.

On the surface, the effect of Jesus' actions is simply to disrupt the system of sacrifice necessarily carried on in the temple.[26] Historically, the sellers were those trading in animals used for sacrifice. The buyers were the pilgrims in need of these animals. The money-changers were the ones whose task it was to convert the Greek or Roman currency the pilgrims brought with them into the Tyrian coinage prescribed for use in the temple and for paying the temple tax. Those selling doves were the persons providing the offering stipulated by law for particular transgressions and rites of purification. And for Jesus to block the passage of goods through the court of the gentiles is for him to call halt to the buying and selling there.

At a deeper level, however, what Jesus is about comes to light in his teaching and in the reaction of the chief priests and the scribes (11:17-18). Through his teaching, Jesus charges that the authorities have profaned the temple by perverting the purpose God intended the court of the gentiles to serve—to be a place of prayer for gentiles—and turning it into a safe haven for their own corrupt practices. Indeed, because of them the temple, Jesus intimates, faces destruction (see Jer. 7:8-15).[27] By delivering this scathing attack in the temple, Jesus thus dares to challenge the authorities in the place that serves as the seat of their rule and to strike at the foundation of their position, privilege, and power.

Thoroughly antagonized by Jesus, the chief priests and the scribes react by wanting to find some way to destroy him (11:18). At the moment, however, they make no move against him for fear of the crowd, who is amazed at Jesus' teaching. Nevertheless, the utterly serious nature of the threat the authorities believe Jesus poses for both them and Israel because of his actions in the temple becomes fully apparent later: As Jesus stands trial, the main charge on which the authorities unsuccessfully attempt to sentence him to death is that he said he would destroy the temple (14:57-58). Moreover, as Jesus hangs on the cross, the passers-by also pick up on this false charge, taunting Jesus: "Aha! You who destroy the temple and build it in three days . . ." (15:29). Ironically, the moment Jesus dies a supernatural portent suddenly occurs foreshadowing the temple's destruction: God tears the curtain of the temple from top to bottom in two (15:38).[28]

With the cleansing of the temple still fresh in their minds, the authorities confront Jesus the following day. Approaching him walking in the temple, the chief priests, scribes, and elders, those who make up the Sanhedrin, bluntly interrogate him about the source of his authority (11:27-33). By whom, they want to know, has he been given authority to do "these things"? The expression "these things" refers most immediately to the cleansing of the temple. Strictly speaking, however, the latter was but one event. From the standpoint of the reader, therefore, the expression "these things" assumes a broader meaning and becomes a reference to the whole of Jesus' ministry. Accordingly, the authorities' question becomes programmatic within Mark's story, for it penetrates to the heart of their entire conflict with Jesus: On whose authority does he act? Because the moment has not yet arrived in Mark's story for Jesus to affirm openly that he is the Son of God acting on the authority of God, he outwits the authorities by answering their question with a counterquestion: How do they view the baptism (ministry) of John? Was it or was it not divinely authorized? Trapped, the authorities cannot answer, for either way they lose. Because they did not submit to John's baptism, they have no desire to expose themselves to the charge of unbelief by ascribing divine authority to John. Because the crowd in the temple holds John to have been a prophet sent by God, they are afraid to deny John divine authority. Since the authorities give Jesus no answer to his question, neither does he give them an answer to their question.

Jesus' refusal to answer the authorities' question straightout, however, does not mean that he simply leaves it dangling.

On the contrary, he does reply to it but couches his reply in the form of the parable of the wicked husbandmen (12:1-12). In this parable, Jesus identifies God, as we noted in the last chapter, as the owner of the vineyard and himself as the son of the owner. Similarly, he identifies the chief priests, scribes, and elders as the tenant farmers whom the owner has entrusted with the care of his vineyard. When the son is at last sent by his father to the farmers, they take him, kill him, and throw him out of the vineyard. By narrating this parable and making these identifications, Jesus advances the claim that contains within it the answer to the question the authorities asked: Sent by God to Israel, he is the Son of God acting on the authority of God, and they will kill him. In figurative speech, therefore, Jesus affirms before members of the Sanhedrin that the one who has given him the authority to do "these things" is God. Because the authorities understand the claim Jesus has made, they want to arrest him immediately. Because they fear the crowd, they hold back. And because they categorically reject the notion that Jesus is the Son of God acting on the authority of God, they remain blind to both the mystery of his person and the source of his authority.

Next, some of the Pharisees and Herodians take their turn at matching wits with Jesus. Sent by the members of the Sanhedrin, they search Jesus out to ensnare him in his speech (12:13-17). Hypocritically, they flatter him as one who correctly teaches the kind of life pleasing to God. Unknowingly, they have, of course, spoken the truth. Nevertheless, their question concerns taxes: Is it lawful to pay the poll-tax to Caesar, or not? In their question lies their trap, for regardless of whether Jesus answers "Yes" or "No," they will have caught him. If he answers, "Yes," he risks being seen by Jews as elevating Caesar above God. If he answers, "No," he risks being seen by the Romans as a revolutionary. Asking them for a coin bearing the image of Caesar, Jesus escapes the trap by answering neither "Yes" nor "No": To do one's duty to Caesar does not, he asserts, contradict doing one's duty to God.[29]

No sooner do the Pharisees and the Herodians fade from view than the Sadducees step forward with a question meant to stump Jesus (12:18-27). Their question has to do with the resurrection, which they disavow because they do not find it in Moses, and the sole purpose of their question is to hold the very notion of resurrection up to ridicule. In Mosaic law, provision is made for "levirate marriage" (Deut. 25:5-10). If a married man who has a brother dies leaving no son, his brother is obligated to take the dead man's wife and have a son by her so as to perpetuate the name of his dead brother. Concocting a caricature of this provision, the Sadducees ask Jesus whose wife a woman would be in the resurrection given the hypothetical case that she had been the wife of seven brothers, all of whom had died childless. Reacting sharply to the Sadducees' question, Jesus charges them with gross ignorance about both the scriptures and the power of God. Whereas they assume that resurrection life must be construed as something tantamount to an extension of earthly circumstances, in actuality God will fashion it as a totally different mode of existence: In the resurrection, people will neither marry nor be given in marriage, but will be like angels in heaven (12:25).[30] And whereas they deny the sheer reality of resurrection, the book of Moses, which they honor, reveals otherwise (Exod. 3:6): For God to affirm to Moses at the burning bush that he "is" the God of Abraham, Isaac, and Jacob proves that these patriarchs, long dead by Moses' time, nonetheless "live." In short, the Sadducees, contends Jesus, know nothing about either the "nature" or the "fact" of resurrection life.

For all intents and purposes, Jesus' controversy with the Sadducees brings to an end the conflict he has with the religious authorities in the temple. To be sure, one more exchange follows. But although this exchange has the form of a controversy, in substance it is a dialogue with a scribe that is devoid of animus though not irony (12:28-34). Having noticed that Jesus answered the Sadducees well, a scribe walks up to him and asks which of all the commandments is foremost. Jesus' reply is that the first of the commandments is love of God and that the second is love of neighbor (Deut. 6:4-5; Lev. 19:18). Unequivocally, the scribe declares Jesus to be right. Jesus, in turn, acknowledges the wisdom he perceives in the scribe, asserting: "You are not far from the kingdom of God." At this, Mark himself signals the end of Jesus' controversies in the temple by remarking, "And after that no one dared to ask him any question" (12:34).

Three things stand out in this pericope. The first is the message Jesus' dialogue with the scribe conveys to the reader of Mark's story: To keep the law or to do God's will is, in essence, to love God and the neighbor. This is true worship, more than all burnt offerings and sacrifices. The second thing is the aura of irony surrounding the figure of the scribe: On the one hand, it is exactly as one who is himself from among the religious authorities that he attests that Jesus, not his fellow authorities, possesses a superior knowledge of the will of God. On the other hand, it is also as one who Jesus says is "not far" from the kingdom that he becomes emblematic of "what could have been the case": Had the religious authorities not denied the divine authority on which Jesus acts and found in him God's agent instead of Satan's agent, they would not now be entangled in conspiracy to kill him but would have heard his gospel calling to repentance and to life in the sphere of God's rule. And the third thing that stands out is the comment with which Mark concludes this pericope (12:34c): By the end of the conflict in the temple, Jesus has reduced all the authorities to silence. Daring no more to try to get the best of Jesus in debate, the authorities withdraw and do not appear again in the story until actively seeking how to arrest and kill him (14:1). The climax of Mark's story is close at hand.

Prior to his passion and before leaving the temple for good, Jesus utters, while still teaching the crowd, one final warning envisaging the scribes (12:38-40). The crowd, he exhorts, is to beware of the scribes, for they strive after the praise not of God but of humans, and their worship of God only masks a total lack of compassion for the poor. Put otherwise, Jesus' caustic complaint against the scribes is that, at bottom, they are hypocritical and deceitful, for they love neither God nor the neighbor. Within Mark's story, this harsh description of the scribes or authorities is the one the reader has in sight as Mark begins the account of Jesus' passion.

Conflict Leading to Death

The passion account (chaps. 14–16) constitutes the culmination of Mark's story and Jesus' death and resurrection the fundamental resolution of Jesus' conflict with Israel. In the opening setting (14:1-2), Mark alerts the reader to this final movement toward culmination and resolution. The comment that the Passover festival (which is the same as the weeklong Feast of Unleavened Bread)[31] occurs within two days[32] reminds the reader that Jesus' "week in Jerusalem" began with his triumphal entry (11:11) and that it is now Wednesday (14:1).[33] The further comment that the chief priests and the scribes, though fearing an uproar among the crowd, seek how they might arrest and kill Jesus echoes earlier passages to this effect extending as far back as the beginning of Jesus' Galilean ministry (12:12; 11:18; 3:6). And like the passion predictions,[34] this comment also focuses attention on who, at the human level, the key players in the passion account are: Jesus and the religious authorities.

Mark is at pains to report that it is "by deceit" that the chief priests and the scribes undertake to bring about the arrest and death of Jesus (14:1). Throughout the passion account, the religious authorities exemplify the negative quality of deceitfulness. Correspondingly, they also show that they themselves are deluded. The result is that the character traits most typical of the authorities in the passion account are those of being deceitful and deluded.

On the one hand, the authorities practice deceit in dealing with others. They gladly accept Judas' offer to betray Jesus and promise him money (14:10-11). To seize Jesus, they arm and send with Judas the selfsame crowd whom Jesus had daily taught in the temple (14:43, 48-49). At Jesus' trial, they try unsuccessfully to convict him through the use of false witnesses, whose credibility Jesus impugns by remaining silent

(14:55-61). At Jesus' hearing before Pilate, they resort to deceit three more times to work their will: When Jesus answers in the affirmative Pilate's question whether he is the King of the Jews, they falsely accuse him of "many things," that is, acts of sedition (15:1-5). Although they feign concern for "law and order" in delivering Jesus to Pilate, in reality they are motivated by envy (15:10). And as Pilate attempts to entice the crowd to choose pardon for Jesus as opposed to the insurrectionist and murderer Barabbas, they manipulate the crowd so it will request release for Barabbas and crucifixion for Jesus (15:6-15).

On the other hand, the authorities show that they themselves are deluded, unable to perceive reality aright. This is especially apparent in connection with Jesus' trial and crucifixion. In both cases, the issue of "authority" stands out prominently. At Jesus' trial before the Sanhedrin, the high priest suddenly asks him whether he is the Messiah, the Son of the Blessed [God]; in reply, Jesus boldly affirms, "I am!" (14:61-62). This claim to be the Son of God (i.e., one sent by God who is uniquely endowed with his authority) is, we recall, the very one Jesus advanced in narrating his parable of the wicked husbandmen to chief priests, scribes, and elders, that is, to members of the Sanhedrin (12:6; 11:27). Confronted with this claim on that occasion, the latter wanted to arrest him at once (12:12). Confronted with this claim on this occasion, they, led by the high priest, condemn him to death for blaspheming God (14:63-64): In their eyes, Jesus has spuriously arrogated to himself the authority and majesty of God. The irony, however, is that in repudiating Jesus' claim on behalf of himself, they unwittingly repudiate the claim that God has made on his behalf and put to death the Son whom God has empowered and sent them (1:11; 9:7; 12:1-9).

As Jesus hangs suffering on the cross, the religious authorities again exhibit the same sort of delusion. Picking up on the inscription citing the charge for which Jesus was crucified, they mock him as the Messiah, the King of Israel (15:31-32). Taunting Jesus, they say to one another, "He saved others, he cannot save himself." This is the last scene in which the authorities appear in Mark's story. In their perspective, Jesus' crucifixion proves that he, in fact, is the one who is "without authority" and that they are the ones who have triumphed in conflict with him. The truth of the matter, however, is that in so thinking, they reveal that they are blind to the reality that Jesus is Israel's Messiah-King exactly as the one who willingly submits to suffering so as to save not himself but others (15:16-20).

In Jesus' death and resurrection, his conflict with the religious authorities comes to fundamental resolution. Utterly convinced they are doing the will of God, the authorities do whatever is necessary to bring Jesus to the cross (2:7; 14:64). As they see it, Jesus is the agent of Satan (3:22) and a menace to Israel's existence because he pits his authority against theirs, threatens to woo the crowd away from them, and violates law, tradition, and the sanctity of the temple. The tragic irony, however, is that in opposing Jesus they unwittingly oppose God and effect their own demise as Israel's leaders (12:9). By raising Jesus from the dead (16:6) and exalting him to universal rule,[35] God vindicates Jesus and shows that he was in the right in his conflict with the authorities. Moreover, God also establishes Jesus' death as the basis of a new covenant whereby atonement for sins is accomplished once for all (14:24; 10:45). The upshot is that Jesus, the crucified and resurrected Son of God (12:6-11), supersedes the temple as the "place" of salvation (15:38) and becomes the one who founds, and presides over, the end-time people of God (14:28; 16:7). As Mark's story draws to a close, therefore, Jesus' cross becomes the symbol, not of his destruction at the hands of the authorities and Pilate, but of the salvation God accomplishes in him on behalf of all humankind.

If Jesus' death and resurrection constitute the fundamental resolution of Jesus' conflict with the religious authorities, the final resolution of this conflict will not occur until Jesus returns at the end of the age. When asked by the high priest at his trial if he is the Messiah, the Son of the Blessed [God], Jesus not only answers, "I am!" but also goes on to predict that one day soon the authorities will see him sitting at the right hand of God and coming with the clouds of heaven (14:61-62). Implicit in Jesus' prediction is the threat of end-time judgment. The point he makes is that because the high priest has asked him whether he is God's Son to condemn him to death (14:55), he can promise the authorities that they will see him yet one more time: At the end of the age, he will return as "the man" God has appointed to be Judge of all and therefore also of them. When Jesus dies on the cross, the authorities are certain that the triumph in their conflict with him has gone to them. The irony is that when Jesus returns as Judge at the end of time, they will behold with their eyes that he is the one whom God has in reality vindicated and put in the right.

Summary

Jesus' conflict with Israel and especially the religious authorities is the pivot on which the plot of Mark's story turns. Since Jesus is the protagonist and they are the antagonists, their story is closely correlated with his.

At the root of Jesus' conflict with the religious authorities is the issue of authority. Mark characterizes Jesus as the Son of God in whom God in his end-time rule draws near and who therefore acts on the authority of God. Jesus is the one who always "thinks the things of God." Mark characterizes the religious authorities as being "without authority." They are the ones who always, with the exception of the friendly scribe, "think the things of humans."

As Jesus' conflict with the religious authorities unfolds, it becomes progressively more intense. In the middle of Mark's story (1:14—8:26), three factors in particular attest to this: (*a*) the comment Mark makes after only the first cycle of controversies that the Pharisees and the Herodians go off and begin consultations on how to destroy Jesus (3:6); (*b*) the overall trend in the controversies from indirect confrontation with Jesus or the disciples to direct confrontation with Jesus whereby he is challenged to prove the legitimacy of his own actions; and (*c*) the parallel trend in the controversies according to which the emphasis shifts from questions having to do with blasphemy, tradition, and Mosaic law to the question about authority itself. Still, one must also note that, in one respect, the conflict between Jesus and the authorities is as grave at the beginning as at the end: The first charge the authorities make against Jesus, committing blasphemy against God, is also the charge for which they finally condemn him to death.

In the long end section of Mark's story (8:27—16:8), Jesus' conflict with the religious authorities prior to his passion takes place principally in the temple (11:27—12:34). If the conflict in the middle of the story is intense, the conflict in the temple is still more intense. To signal this, Mark employs various devices, to wit: The setting of the temple itself intensifies the conflict, for it is both the place of God's presence and the seat of the authorities' rule. The atmosphere in which Jesus' controversies in the temple take place is one of extreme hostility, as the authorities become so irate that they want to destroy him or to seize him on the spot. The controversies themselves are acutely confrontational: Jesus is himself challenged by the authorities on matters pertaining specifically to him. Correspondingly, the questions disputed are all critical in nature: They touch on such matters of authority as the right by which Jesus cleanses the temple, discharges his ministry, and interprets Mosaic law. Uninterruptedly on a single day, all the groups that together make up the united front of the religious authorities approach Jesus so as to oppose him or defeat him in debate. And last, the authorities, having been reduced by Jesus to silence and losing all heart to debate him further, withdraw so as to pursue actively a way by which to have him arrested and killed.

The fundamental resolution of Jesus' conflict with the religious authorities comes in the passion account, with Jesus' death and resurrection (chaps. 14—16). To bring Jesus to the cross, the authorities practice deceit: They use Judas, who betrays Jesus; they manipulate the crowd into assisting in

Jesus' arrest and calling for Barabbas's release and Jesus' crucifixion; and they falsely accuse Jesus before Pilate. As they
see it, Jesus must die, for he acts on the authority of Satan,
undermines their authority, threatens to woo the crowd away
from them, and opposes law, tradition, and temple. Despite
their cunning, however, the authorities reveal that they themselves are deluded and incapable of discerning the true nature
of things. Ironically, in the firm belief that they know the
mind of God and are doing his will, they unwittingly oppose
God by repudiating the Son and King he has sent them. In
point of fact, as they witness Jesus hanging on the cross, they
are convinced he has been stripped of all authority and that
the victory in their conflict with him has gone to them. In
reality, however, God intervenes on behalf of his Son Jesus,
raises him from the dead and thus puts him in the right in
his conflict with them, and exalts him to the position of authority over all. Indeed, under the hand of God all of the
following occur: The death of Jesus Son of God becomes the
means whereby atonement for sins is accomplished once for
all; Jesus himself supersedes the temple as the "place" of
salvation; and Jesus becomes the founder and ruler of God's
end-time people. Nonetheless, not included in Mark's story
is yet another decisive occurrence constituting the final resolution of his story: At the end of the age, Jesus Son of God
will return in splendor to gather the elect and decide the fate
of all people. At this time, the religious authorities, who have
so bitterly opposed Jesus, will see with their eyes what they
have otherwise refused to perceive: that Jesus is in truth the
Son of God and bearer of God's kingdom, the one who acts
on the authority of God.

4

The Story of the
DISCIPLES

*E*ntwined with the stories of Jesus and the religious authorities is also Mark's story of the disciples.[1] Like the authorities, the disciples make their debut in the middle section (1:14—8:26), after Jesus has been presented. As Jesus commences his public ministry to Israel, he proclaims the gospel of God (1:14-15) and calls his first disciples (1:16-20). Except perhaps for Judas, the disciples do not materially influence the plot, or flow of events, of Mark's story.

We saw in the last chapter that the major conflict of Mark's story is between Jesus and Israel. Because Israel does not receive Jesus as God's supreme agent and the religious authorities see in him a mortal threat to both themselves and the nation, Jesus' conflict with Israel is to the death. In Jesus' cross and resurrection, this conflict comes to fundamental resolution, just as it will come to final resolution in his Parousia. Besides Israel, Jesus also enters into conflict with the disciples. The tenor of this conflict, however, is altogether different, for the disciples are not Jesus' enemies but his followers. Still, to note that this conflict is different is not to suggest that it is trivial. On the contrary, it revolves around the disciples' remarkable lack of comprehension and their refusal to come to terms with either the central purpose of Jesus' ministry or the true meaning of discipleship. The resolution of this conflict is not narrated by Mark; instead, he leaves it to the reader to project its outcome. To assist the reader in this, however, Mark provides him or her with important clues.

The Call to Discipleship and Incomprehension

The Call to Discipleship

As Mark acquaints the reader with the disciples in the middle of his story, he casts them in a positive light. Primarily, Jesus calls the disciples and commissions them to a ministry in Israel.

Embarking on his public ministry, Jesus calls his first disciples, two pairs of brothers: Peter and Andrew (1:16-18); and James and John (1:19-20). Noteworthy is that the call of each pair of brothers conforms to an identical pattern, to wit: (*a*) Underway, (*b*) Jesus sees the brothers, (*c*) calls them, and (*d*) immediately they go after him. By means of this pattern, Mark sets forth the nature and purpose of discipleship.

The nature of discipleship is joining oneself to Jesus in total allegiance. In Mark's portrayal of the calling of disciples, the initiative lies wholly with Jesus: While going his appointed way, Jesus is the one who sees and calls. That Jesus should control the initiative is more striking than first appearances admit. In rabbinic circles, for example, it was the candidate himself who sought out the teacher in the hope of being accepted as his disciple.[2] To stress that the initiative lies with Jesus is to attest to the sovereign authority with which he calls disciples. Correspondingly, the response of those called is immediate acceptance. Dropping their nets, Simon and Andrew follow Jesus at once, just as James and John abandon father, boat, and hired hands. Immediate acceptance is indicative of the absolute obedience with which the brothers receive their call: They leave behind goods, family, and profession to join themselves to Jesus, to follow him wherever he goes, and to give him their undivided loyalty. As Peter remarks later: "Behold, we have left everything and followed you!" (10:28).

The close correspondence between Jesus' summons (e.g., "Come after me," 1:17) and the brothers' acceptance (e.g., "And immediately . . . they followed him," 1:18) reveals that such expressions as to "follow" and to "come [go] after" Jesus, where they entail commitment to him, function in Mark's story as technical terms connoting discipleship. When used as technical terms, "following" and "coming after" Jesus describe those accompanying him as doing so precisely as his disciples.[3] In Mark's story, the disciple is, in effect, one who is a committed follower of Jesus.

This latter point is worth noting because it is not without implications. For one thing, it implies that not all people said to follow Jesus are to be construed as disciples. For example, the crowd, although it follows Jesus (3:7; 5:24), is nonetheless not to be pictured as a huge throng of disciples, for it is not committed to Jesus in a bond of allegiance.[4] For another thing, this point also implies that discipleship is not a privilege restricted exclusively to the twelve. To be sure, when Mark refers to Jesus' "disciples," it appears that the twelve are generally the ones envisaged.[5] This notwithstanding, examples of persons outside the circle of the twelve who nevertheless must be accounted as Jesus' disciples are Levi (2:14), "those who were about him" (with the twelve) (4:10, 34), and the women watching the crucifixion from afar (15:40-41).[6] Accordingly, if the twelve are the most prominent of the disciples of Jesus, this is not to say that beyond the pale of the twelve Jesus is without disciples.

The purpose of discipleship is announced by Jesus in his call to Simon and Andrew: "Come after me, and I shall make you become fishers of men" (1:17). Plainly, discipleship has "mission work" as its purpose. Striking is the universal nature of the mission Jesus envisages. At this juncture in Mark's story, Jesus is just beginning his ministry to Israel. Already, however, his vision encompasses not only the pre-Easter mission of the disciples to Israel (6:7-13) but also their post-Easter mission to the nations (13:10; 14:9).

As the first disciples called, Peter, Andrew, James, and John become, in varying degrees, representative of the twelve. This is true especially of Peter, who stands out as the spokesman[7] of the twelve and the one who is typical[8] of them both in greatness and in weakness. On one occasion, John too serves as spokesman for the twelve (9:38), and on another James and John become typical of them (10:35-45). Three times Jesus singles out Peter, James, and John to share some special experience with him, such as the raising of Jairus's daughter (5:37), his transfiguration (9:2), or his agony in Gethsemane (14:33-34); and it is at the request of Peter, James, John, and Andrew that Jesus delivers his eschatological discourse (13:3-4). Although unquestionably situated within the circle of the twelve, the first disciples function variously as stand-ins for the entire group.

The call of Levi is guided by the same pattern as the call of Peter, Andrew, James, and John. Passing by along the sea, Jesus sees Levi the son of Alphaeus sitting at the tax office, calls him, and Levi gets up and follows Jesus (2:14). In the call of Levi, therefore, Mark narrates the call of a true disciple.

This formal parallelism between Levi's call and that of the first disciples creates the expectation that Levi's name too will appear in the list of the twelve (3:16-19). Surprisingly, however, it does not. Among the names of the twelve, one does encounter James the son of Alphaeus (3:18). But of any link between James and Levi, Mark says nary a word. Given the sparse data Mark provides, one does best to infer that although Levi is a true disciple, he is not one of the twelve.[9]

Less obscure is the reason Mark highlights Jesus' call of Levi. Levi is a toll collector (2:14). As such, he is a member of a class notorious for its dishonesty and scorned by fellow Jews.[10] To depict the summons of a toll collector to discipleship is to show that Jesus joins to himself not only upright persons like Peter, Andrew, James, and John but also those like Levi who are disreputable. As Jesus says to the Pharisees, "I came not to call the righteous but sinners" (2:17).

At the time Jesus calls Levi, he is already embroiled in the first cycle of controversies with the religious leaders (2:1—3:6). At the end of this cycle, Mark reports that the Pharisees take leave to conspire on how to destroy Jesus (3:6). On another note, news of Jesus has also circulated so widely that a great crowd from all parts of Palestine and from Tyre and Sidon streams to him (3:7-8). After healing their sick, Jesus withdraws to a mountain, and here he creates the twelve.

As the setting for the creation of the twelve, the mountain is itself significant (3:13). In Mark's story world, the mountain connotes nearness to God and is therefore a place of divine-human communication and encounter.[11] Atop a mountain, Jesus prays (6:46), is transfigured by God (9:2-8), and foretells the future (13:3-5). Just as God once established Israel from atop a mountain (Exodus 19–20), so Jesus, also atop a mountain, establishes the end-time people of God.[12]

Mark couches his narration of Jesus' creation of the twelve in a pattern similar to the one he employs in the call stories. In so doing, Mark stresses the incomparable authority with which Jesus acts and the absolute obedience with which his call is received. In creating the twelve, Jesus himself takes the initiative ("he himself called to him those whom he desired," 3:13). In response to Jesus' call, those summoned come to him at once ("and they went away to him," 3:13). Having chosen the twelve, Jesus also commissions them. The commission he gives them is dual: The twelve are to be "with him" and to be sent to "preach and to cast out demons" (3:14-16). In that the twelve are "with Jesus," they live in the sphere of God's inbreaking rule and become eye- and ear-witnesses to his ministry.[13] In that they preach and cast out demons, they are empowered by Jesus to do as he has been doing; their activity is an extension of his.

By formally citing the names of the twelve, Mark shows that the circle of the twelve is now complete. Jesus continues to call disciples (8:34; 10:21), but the group of twelve remains fixed. In giving Simon the surname "Peter" and in describing Judas Iscariot as the one "who also betrayed him," Mark alerts the reader to both the preferred name that Simon will henceforth bear and the sinister role that Judas will later play (3:16, 19).

In recounting the creation of the twelve, Mark has already laid the groundwork for describing the ministry to Israel they will undertake. Before turning to this, however, Mark enriches significantly his characterization of Jesus' disciples. Within the context of Jesus' discourse in parables, Mark reports that Jesus says to "those about him with the twelve": "To you is given the secret of the kingdom of God, but for those outside everything is in parables" (4:10-11). The contrast Jesus makes in these words between "disciples" and "outsiders" could not be starker: On the one hand, God imparts to the disciples enlightenment and understanding concerning the secret of his end-time rule; on the other hand, outsiders stand before this secret as before a riddle.

In the parables that Jesus narrates in his discourse[11] and explains to his disciples (4:34), he indicates how the secret of God's kingdom, or end-time rule, is to be understood.[15] This secret is that God's end-time rule is a present, albeit hidden, reality, straining toward its consummation at the close of the age. In Jesus, God in his end-time rule draws near so as to confront humans.[16] In particular, Jesus proclaims the gospel of God and summons Israel to repentance, to belief in the gospel, and to life in the sphere of God's rule.[17] While some have heard Jesus' message (indeed, with astonishing results! 4:8), it has otherwise fallen on deaf ears (4:3-7). For example, the religious authorities have heard Jesus' message and witnessed his works, yet far from seeing in them signs of the presence of God's rule, they are convinced Jesus is the agent of Satan (3:22, 30). God's rule, therefore, is a hidden reality. Nevertheless, from such insignificant beginnings as the ministry of Jesus, God's rule will grow, until at the end of the age it will, as a consummated reality, encompass the world (4:26-29, 30-32).

Following the parable discourse, Mark tells of Jesus' trip across the sea and back, of two healings, and of Jesus' rejection in Nazareth. Then he pictures Jesus as widening his ministry: In renewing the commission he gave the twelve,[18] Jesus sends them out into Israel on a ministry of their own (6:7-13, 30). As Mark describes the renewal of the twelve's commission, the same emphases so prominent in earlier call stories reappear even while new ones also emerge. Thus, the initiative once again lies wholly with Jesus: Jesus summons the twelve, sends them out two by two, empowers them to have authority over unclean spirits, and gives them instructions for the way. Specifically, Jesus charges the twelve to take nothing but a staff for self-defense; to journey only in sandals or light footwear; not to weigh themselves down by wearing more than one garment; to rely on the hospitality of those they meet for the necessities of food, shelter, and the things money buys; to stay in only one house in any given place until time to leave that place; and to shake the dust off their feet as a warning of judgment against the residents of any place refusing to receive them or to hear their message (6:8-11). In short, the twelve are to travel lightly and to keep on the move as they carry out their ministry, trusting in God to provide for them.

In willing obedience, the twelve undertake the mission Jesus entrusts to them (6:12-13, 30). Their ministry is clearly an extension of his, for as they journey through Israel they do exactly as he has done: They proclaim the message of repentance,[19] teach,[20] heal,[21] and cast out demons.[22] The one thing they do that Mark has not attributed to Jesus is anoint the sick with oil, a gesture symbolizing the healing with which God visits the sick (6:13).[23] Significantly, when the twelve return to Jesus and recount all they have done and taught, Mark refers to them neither as the twelve nor as disciples but as "the apostles" (6:30). In their ministry to Israel, the twelve stand out as Jesus' messengers, or ambassadors: Receiving them is tantamount to receiving Jesus himself (9:37).

Incomprehension

As sketched thus far, Mark's portrait of the disciples could not be more favorable. Called by Jesus to follow him, they have responded in obedience, leaving behind former ways of life and committing themselves to his cause by giving him their allegiance and undivided loyalty. Still, the impression that all is well with the disciples is deceptive, for already the prospect of conflict between Jesus and them looms large.

The cardinal problem besetting the disciples is incomprehension. At first blush, this in itself seems baffling. Yet, Mark's characterization of the disciples is that despite their "being with" Jesus, they still do not comprehend aright. To be with Jesus is to learn of him, to "think the things of God, not of humans." The disciples, however, show themselves prone to regard reality from a human point of view. Hence, their incomprehension.

From the standpoint of both Mark as narrator and Jesus, the disciples, in failing to comprehend aright, are without excuse. As the reader well knows, it is not as though Jesus has not initiated the disciples in "thinking the things of God." On the contrary, from early on in Mark's story the disciples are eye- and ear-witnesses as Jesus teaches, preaches, exorcises demons, and heals with incomparable authority.[24] Also, through the parables that Jesus narrates and explains (4:34) they are given the secret that in Jesus, God in his end-time rule has drawn near and will in the future usher in his glorious kingdom (4:11). Furthermore, in choosing the twelve, Jesus likewise endows them with divine authority (3:14-15). In short, one does not have far to read in Mark's story before all the conditions are right for the disciples to view Jesus, his ministry, and themselves from a divine point of view; they are in a position to comprehend that Jesus is God's supreme agent (the Messiah Son of God [1:1]) who discharges his ministry on divine authority and has endowed them too with authority. Regardless, because of their proclivity to think in human terms, the disciples show in the latter half of the middle of Mark's story that they comprehend neither who Jesus is nor what it is either to trust his authority or to avail themselves of the authority granted them.

A first indication of the disciples' incomprehension occurs already in the very context in which Jesus declares the disciples enlightened by God about the secret of his end-time rule (4:11). Asked by the disciples about his parables after narrating that of the sower, Jesus retorts, "Do you not understand this parable? How then will you understand all the parables?" (4:13). To be sure, Jesus explains the parable of the sower to the disciples,[25] just as he does his other parables as well (4:34). This notwithstanding, he expects them to comprehend the parables and they do not. Indeed, to preclude any misconception about this, Mark replicates this scene later. Asked by the disciples another time about a parable, Jesus answers in reproach, "Then are you also without understanding?" (7:18).

These brief scenes reflect the pattern that prevails in Jesus' relationship with the disciples in the latter half of the middle of Mark's story: Jesus anticipates comprehension on the part of the disciples and they exhibit a profound lack thereof. The upshot is that conflict erupts between Jesus and the disciples, and nowhere is this more apparent than in a series of three boat scenes and two feeding miracles, with the miracles interspersed among the boat scenes.

The first boat scene occurs immediately following Jesus' discourse in parables (4:35-41). Prior to this discourse, Jesus had ordered the disciples to ready a boat (3:9),[26] and it was from the boat that he delivered the discourse (4:1). The discourse ended, Jesus summons the disciples to sail eastward across the Sea of Galilee (4:35). While he retires to the stern to sleep, the disciples encounter a fierce storm. With waves beating against the boat and the boat filling with water, the disciples become terrified. They arouse Jesus, appealing to him for rescue, and he rebukes the wind and silences the water in a manner reminiscent of his exorcising demons. The ensuing calm enables the disciples to complete their voyage, but not before the following exchange takes place. Jesus chides the disciples: "Why are you so cowardly? Have you still no faith?"[27] (4:40); and the disciples, in turn, query one another: "Who then is this, that even wind and sea obey him?"

In this scene, the disciples attest to their incomprehension by adopting a human, not divine, view of their situation out on the water. Although the disciples have heretofore observed Jesus perform powerful acts on numerous occasions, they are nonetheless without faith, or trust, in his divine authority to see them through this peril. Moreover, the question the disciples pose about Jesus' identity shows that despite his calming the fierce storm, they perceive no revelation in this that he is God's Son. The fear gripping the disciples is no sign of reverence for Jesus but is symptomatic of their incomprehension.

After a brief stay on the gentile side of the Sea of Galilee, Jesus and the disciples return westward to the Jewish side. The disciples witness more of Jesus' ministry, and are themselves empowered and sent out to minister in Israel (5:1—6:30). Upon their return, Jesus takes the disciples away by boat to a deserted place so that they may refresh themselves. The crowd, however, spots Jesus and the disciples leaving and is present to meet them when they land (6:31-33). This is the setting for the first feeding miracle.

The substance of this miracle is that Jesus feeds five thousand men, manifesting himself not only as authoritative Son of God but also as Israel's Shepherd-King (6:34-44). Late in the day, after Jesus has taught the crowd, the disciples approach him with an eminently sensible suggestion: Send the crowd away so that all can buy themselves something to eat. Ignoring the disciples' suggestion, Jesus challenges them to feed the crowd: "You give them something to eat" (6:37). To the disciples, Jesus' directive means that he would have them rather than the crowd go off and purchase the necessary food. Still, when they propose this, Jesus ignores this suggestion too. Instead, he asks about the provisions they have with them, and when told they have five loaves and two fishes, he himself takes command of the situation. Blessing the loaves and dividing the two fish, Jesus has the disciples distribute them to the crowd. After all five thousand eat and are satisfied, the disciples gather up twelve baskets of bread and pieces of fish.

In this episode too, the disciples amply manifest their incomprehension. Immediately prior to this miracle, Jesus endowed the disciples with authority to discharge their mission in Israel, and they completed it (6:7-13, 30). Against this backdrop, Jesus now challenges the disciples to feed the five thousand. He anticipates that they will avail themselves of the authority earlier granted them and do so. In other words, Jesus expects the disciples to face this challenge by "thinking the things of God." The disciples, however, prove themselves oblivious to all that has preceded. Consequently, they face the challenge "thinking the things of humans." Assessing the situation from a human point of view, they show by their remarks that they comprehend neither that Jesus has the authority to feed the crowd nor that he has endowed them with such authority.

The second boat scene follows the feeding of the five thousand (6:45-52). Compelling the disciples to board the boat, Jesus has them set sail without him for Bethsaida on the east side of the sea. Toward evening, as he stands on land, he sees the disciples hard pressed at rowing, struggling against a contrary wind. Later, about three o'clock in the morning, he comes to them walking on the water, intending to pass them by. If Jesus' "passing by" alludes to the OT motif of God's passing by, then Jesus' intention is to reveal himself to the disciples as God's authoritative Son who saves.[28] Seeing Jesus, however, the disciples believe they have caught sight of a ghost and cry out in terror. Immediately, Jesus calms them: "Take courage," he says, "it is I; have no fear!" (6:50). With this, Jesus gets into the boat and the wind abates. At the conclusion of the scene, Mark himself comments: "And they were utterly astounded, for they did not understand about the loaves, but their hearts were hardened" (6:51-52).

For the reader, the key to interpreting this scene lies in Mark's comment. In it, Mark alludes to the miraculous feeding of the five thousand. There, we remember, Jesus had the disciples assist him as he performed the miracle. Regardless of their participation, however, Mark lets it be known that the disciples are still unable to view the miracle in divine terms and view it only in human terms: They still have no grasp of Jesus' divine authority or that he revealed himself through the miracle to be God's Son and Israel's Shepherd-King; and neither do they grasp that they could have done the same thing. Moreover, Mark's comment furthermore tells the reader that the incomprehension afflicting the disciples relative to the feeding of the five thousand also afflicts them in this second boat scene. As Jesus compels the disciples to set sail for Bethsaida, he entrusts them in effect with a mission. The disciples, however, construe their journey, or mission, in purely human terms: Fighting a contrary wind, they do not recall that Jesus has endowed them with authority to complete whatever mission he gives them. And seeing Jesus walk on the water, they cannot imagine his authority would enable this and think instead the image is a ghost. Once more, they are unable to comprehend the situation aright. Instead of trusting, they fear; and they have also become hardened in their incomprehension.

At the end of this second boat scene, Jesus and the disciples land at Gennesaret (6:53), on the west side of the sea. Continuing his ministry for a time in Galilee, Jesus once more travels in gentile regions, where the second feeding miracle takes place (8:1-10). Surrounded by a massive crowd of four thousand that remains with him three days, Jesus summons the disciples and tells them he has compassion on the people because they have nothing to eat. Confounded, the disciples simply ask, "How can one feed these people with bread here in the desert?" (8:4). As before, Jesus' response is to inquire of them about the food they have. When they reply, "Seven [loaves]," Jesus takes, blesses, and breaks the loaves, and gives them to the disciples to set before the people; similarly, he also distributes a few small fish. After having fed to satisfaction all four thousand persons, the disciples gather up seven baskets full of scraps.

Essentially, the interaction between Jesus and the disciples in this miracle concerning four thousand gentiles is the same as in the previous miracle concerning five thousand Jews. Challenged by Jesus with the task of feeding the hungry crowd, the disciples, seemingly untouched by their previous experiences out on the sea or with the crowd of five thousand, are at a loss to do anything but express their utter perplexity. Once again, Jesus would have them view the situation from his divine point of view, but they view it from a human point of view. Jesus would have them comprehend the nature of his authority, perceive in it that he is God's powerful Son, and recall that he has also empowered them for ministry. In short, Jesus would have them perform the miracle. They, however, understand none of these things, and even though they assist Jesus as he performs the miracle, they still remain uncomprehending.

Back again in Galilee, Jesus and the disciples are approached by the Pharisees who demand that Jesus give them a sign to prove God is at work in his ministry. Refusing the Pharisees their sign, Jesus reboards the boat with the disciples and sails in a northeasterly direction, eventually landing at Bethsaida. This journey provides the setting for the third boat scene.

This third boat scene (8:14-21) opens with the spotlight on the disciples. Because they forgot to bring food, they have only one loaf among them and this bothers them greatly. While they busy themselves expressing their consternation over this, Jesus tries unsuccessfuly to warn them of the evil influence of the Pharisees and Herod. Ignored by the disciples, Jesus becomes exasperated. In language with which he has otherwise characterized only "outsiders" (4:11-12), he roundly scolds the disciples: "Do you not yet perceive or understand?" "Are your hearts hardened? Having eyes do you not see, and having ears do you not hear? And do you not remember?" (8:17-18). The remembering Jesus has in mind refers to the two feeding miracles, and he mentions them both. Then he concludes with a final question: "Do you not yet understand?" (8:21).

This third boat scene is climactic in emphasizing the incomprehension of the disciples. By citing the feeding miracles and addressing such matters as lack of perception, hardened hearts, and the failure to remember, Jesus' words recapitulate the substance of the three boat scenes and the two feeding miracles. Despite auspicious beginnings, the disciples, by the end of this series of scenes and miracles, show themselves to be like "outsiders." Like "outsiders," they "think the things not of God, but of humans" and regard reality from a this-worldly point of view. Of course, unlike "outsiders," the disciples follow Jesus and are "with him" in commitment to his cause. Accordingly, incomprehension on the one hand and commitment on the other are hallmark traits of the disciples.

Jesus' struggle with them is to lead them to overcome their incomprehension lest it undermine their commitment to him. This is the central issue in Jesus' relationship with the disciples, and this third boat scene highlights it vividly.

Mark concludes the middle of his story (1:14—8:26) by portraying Jesus as healing a blind man (8:22-26). Noteworthy is that the healing takes place in two stages: After Jesus first lays his hands on the man's eyes, the man sees people but they look like trees. After Jesus lays his hands on the man's eyes a second time, the man is completely healed and sees everything clearly. Is this miracle paradigmatic of Jesus' struggle with the disciples? Is Jesus' earthly ministry stage one, during which time Jesus must contend with the disciples who are at once committed to him but afflicted with incomprehension? Is the time following Easter stage two, when Jesus shall have led the disciples, like this man, to "see everything clearly"?

To sum up, in the middle of his story (1:14—8:26) Mark first describes the call of the disciples and then concentrates on their fundamental character flaw, incomprehension. In the first half of the middle of his story, Mark tells of the call of the first disciples, of the creation of the twelve, and of the ministry of the twelve in Israel. Although the number of Jesus' disciples is greater than twelve, the twelve nevertheless epitomize the disciples. In the call to discipleship, the initiative lies wholly with Jesus: He sees, and he summons. Those who hear his summons leave behind former ways of life, follow him by giving him their undivided loyalty, and are "with him" as eye- and ear-witnesses to his ministry. Through Jesus, disciples become members of God's end-time people, live in the sphere of his inbreaking rule, and are privy to the secret of this rule. Called to mission, they are empowered and sent by Jesus to Israel; like Jesus, they preach, teach, heal, and exorcise demons. Thus far, Mark's portrait of the disciples is highly favorable.

In the latter half of the middle of his story, Mark casts the disciples in a predominantly negative light. In connection with parables that Jesus utters and in a series of three boat scenes interspersed by two feeding miracles, the disciples are afflicted with incomprehension. Although enlightened by God and empowered by Jesus, they comprehend neither the parables of Jesus nor his identity nor the nature of either his authority or the authority granted them. The result is that they fail badly in situations calling for insight, faith, courage, confession, or action. The reason for the disciples' incomprehension is traceable to the way they construe reality. Although initiated by Jesus in "thinking the things of God," they "think the things of humans" instead. The upshot is that Jesus must struggle not only with Israel but also with them. In their hearts, they are divided: Although they are committed to Jesus, they seem unable to view reality, as he does, in term of God's approaching, end-time rule. Jesus' struggle is to lead the disciples to overcome their incomprehension; should he fail to do so, it will destroy their commitment to him and their new life as his disciples.

Discipleship as Servanthood

In the long end section of his story (8:27—16:8), Mark tells of Jesus as "on the way" to Jerusalem and of his suffering, death, and rising. Intertwined with this story line is the story line of the disciples, in which Mark further develops the motif of their incomprehension.

Overall, the disciples' incomprehension deepens and becomes more directly related to the fate of Jesus. In the middle of the story, the disciples' incomprehension concerns Jesus' parables, his identity, the nature of his authority, and the nature of the authority granted them. Here in the end of the story, their incomprehension concerns the essence of Jesus' ministry and therefore also the essence of discipleship. The essence of Jesus' ministry is defined by his passion predictions and centers on his suffering and death (8:31; 9:31; 10:33-34). The essence of discipleship is defined by Jesus' summons to the crowd and the disciples: "If anyone would come after me, let him deny himself and take up his cross, and let him follow me" (8:34). Accordingly, just as the essence of Jesus' ministry is servanthood, so the essence of discipleship is servanthood. The disciples do not, and in fact will not, comprehend the essence of either Jesus' ministry or discipleship because they persist in "thinking the things not of God, but of humans"; they are not disposed to learn from Jesus the ways of God. Because the stakes get higher as the story progresses, the conflict between Jesus and the disciples becomes more intense. The question the reader must weigh is how, or whether, Jesus can bring the disciples to adopt his divine point of view regarding both his fate and discipleship.

However bleak Mark's story of the disciples appears to be, it is not altogether devoid of positive features. For example, until Jesus' arrest, the disciples continue to follow him and be "with him." Despite their incomprehension, they also solicit him for instruction and hear his words.[29] Indeed, though his confession is insufficient, Peter nonetheless correctly affirms on behalf of the disciples that Jesus is the Messiah (8:29). In Jesus' controversies with the religious authorities, the disciples evince loyalty to him by standing with him.[30] Then too, the disciples are likewise obedient to him, as when he twice sends two of them on important errands, once to obtain the colt on which he will ride into Jerusalem (11:1-7) and once to prepare for the eating of the Passover (14:12-16). Again, as Jesus enters Jerusalem the disciples apparently join with the throng in hailing him as David's greater son with shouts of Hosanna (11:9-10). Moreover, when at meal Jesus foretells that he will be betrayed by one of them, they all (except perhaps Judas) are genuinely grieved by his words (14:17-20). And after thrice denying Jesus, Peter expresses his remorse by breaking down and weeping (14:72).

The Notion of Servanthood Rejected

Jesus' passion predictions set the tone for Mark's portrayal of the disciples in the end of his story (8:27—16:8). This is apparent from the initial section (8:27—10:45), in which Mark develops a pattern that possesses the key elements of passion predication, incomprehension, and instruction. Three times in this section (*a*) Jesus predicts his passion, (*b*) the disciples show by what they do or say that they have not comprehended his prediction, and (*c*) Jesus instructs the disciples in "thinking the things of God" regarding discipleship.

The first occurrence of this pattern is in the subsection 8:27—9:1. The scene that serves as the backdrop against which this pattern unfolds is Peter's confession of Jesus (8:27-30). This scene is startling in its own right, for what the disciples have heretofore not understood, they suddenly, even though insufficiently, do understand: Jesus' identity.

As Jesus is in the regions of Caesarea Philippi on the way to Jerusalem, he abruptly asks the disciples who the Jewish public thinks he is. In reply to the disciples' answer that the public thinks him to be a prophet of some sort, Jesus asks them who they think he is. On behalf of the disciples, Peter declares, "You are the Messiah!" and Jesus immediately commands the disciples to silence about this (8:29-30).

During Jesus' ministry in Israel, the disciples, the reader knows, have witnessed Jesus speak and act with divine authority (1:16—8:26). Despite this, the disciples have remained imperceptive to the revelation conveyed thereby that he is the Messiah Son of God (1:1). Indeed, after Jesus calmed the storm in the first boat scene, the only response the disciples managed was the fearful question: "Who then is this, that even wind and sea obey him?" (4:41). Here near Caesarea Philippi, however, this veil of incomprehension lifts and the disciples suddenly perceive Jesus to be the Messiah. In retrospect, this means they recognize him as God's Anointed, the Messiah-King of Israel who, in teaching, preaching, healing, exorcising demons, calming storms, and feeding the crowd, has been acting on divine authority.

Remarkable as this insight is, we recall from chapter 2 that it is still insufficient. It is insufficient because it both slights the deepest mystery of Jesus' identity—that he is the Son of God (1:11)—and does not envisage the heart of his ministry—suffering and death. Because of the insufficiency of this insight, Jesus commands the disciples to silence (8:30). At the same time, he also uses this insight as a springboard to raise for the first time the matter of his passion.

Jesus' First Passion-Prediction.   In the wake of Peter's confession, Jesus delivers his first passion prediction (8:31). In it, he teaches the disciples that suffering, death, and resurrection will be his fate and that the principal "actors" involved will be God, Jesus himself, and the religious authorities. Instantly, Peter evinces the incomprehension besetting all the disciples by categorically rejecting the notion that Jesus' fate should be death (8:32). Fixing his gaze on all the disciples, Jesus reprimands Peter for serving as Satan's stand-in, that is, for trying to divert him from his divinely appointed goal and hence "thinking the things not of God, but of humans." Then Jesus instructs not only the disciples but also the crowd in the values of discipleship.

In his instruction on discipleship (8:34—9:1), Jesus emphasizes the following points. To come after him as a disciple is to surrender one's own will ("to deny oneself") in favor of giving one's allegiance to him and being prepared, if necessary, even to give one's life for him ("to take up one's cross"; 8:34). To try to secure one's life on one's own terms is ultimately to lose it; to lose one's life in the service of Jesus and the gospel is ultimately to save it (8:35). In the last analysis, discipleship has to do with the utterly precious commodity of "life," and those who deny (or confess) Jesus in this sinful age will be denied (or acknowledged) by him at the end of the age when he returns for judgment (8:36-38). What is more, disciples can also rest assured that they can anticipate seeing in the near future the rule of God come in power and splendor (9:1).[31]

In the scenes following these sayings, the reader is exposed to further examples of both incomprehension and instruction (9:2-29). Atop the high mountain, Jesus is transfigured before Peter, James, and John, and God declares from the cloud, "This is my beloved Son, listen to him!" (9:7). Here God himself "supplements" Peter's earlier confession both by affirming that Jesus is his unique Son and by enjoining the three disciples to attend to Jesus as he teaches them that suffering, death, and resurrection lie before him. Overcome by fear, the three disciples do not comprehend the revelation given to them and, as they descend from the mountain, Jesus commands them to silence about it until after his resurrection (9:5-6, 9). Within Mark's story, Jesus' command is of special importance. It implies that following the resurrection the three disciples will tell of their experience atop the mountain, which is to say that they will also comprehend the revelation that occurred there. After the resurrection, they will comprehend aright both who Jesus is and what he was about. For now, however, the three do as Jesus has just told them: They keep things to themselves even while questioning what Jesus means when he says he will "rise from the dead" (9:10).

Still descending from the mountain, the three disciples ask Jesus why the scribes say that "first Elijah must come" (9:11). This question provides Jesus with the opportunity both to allude to John the Baptist as the one who fulfilled the end-time expectation associated with Elijah and to point out that John's suffering, as attested by scripture, is anticipatory of his own (9:11-13).

Joining the disciples below, Jesus and the three discover that the nine have attempted in vain to cast out an unclean spirit from a man's son (9:14-29). Although Jesus endowed the disciples with authority to cast out demons when he created the twelve and sent them out (3:15; 6:7), the nine do not trust God that they have this authority and consequently are unable to avail themselves of it to perform the miracle (9:28). Jesus' advice that an exorcism like this can be accomplished only through "prayer" is another way of saying that it can be accomplished only through trust in God (9:29). Once again, the disciples have failed because of incomprehension, of "thinking the things not of God, but of humans."

Jesus' Second Passion Prediction.   In the subsection 9:30-50, the reader again encounters the pattern of passion prediction, incomprehension, and instruction. Foretelling his passion, Jesus teaches a second time that he will suffer, be killed, and rise (9:31). Once more, however, the disciples do not comprehend Jesus' prediction, as Mark himself says (9:32). Moreover, the disciples themselves show that Jesus' teaching is lost on them. No sooner has he told them of his ministry—laying down his life—than they become embroiled in a dispute over which of them is greatest (9:33-34). Sitting down and assuming the posture of teacher, Jesus calls the disciples and instructs them at length in the ethics of discipleship (9:35-50).

The key point Jesus makes is paradoxical in nature: Whoever would be "first" (i.e., greatest) must be "last of all," which means becoming "servant of all" (9:35). To exemplify this, Jesus takes a child—one who is without status or power and wholly in need of being served—and ministers to the child by holding the child in his arms, which is a gesture of nurture and caring (9:36). Then, as if to interpret his act, Jesus announces that to render service to another in his name, that is, for no other reason than being his disciple, is in effect to have rendered service both to him and to God (9:37). Having thus made his point, Jesus also asserts through a string of sayings that disciples (and others as well; 9:38-41) lead life only in intimate relation to him (9:41-50). Actions performed "in his name" (i.e., because of him) will not fail of ultimate reward; actions resulting in separation from him will incur final judgment. And as for the twelve themselves, they are not to engage in jealous quarrels over who is greatest but to live in peace with one another (9:50).

Just as in the previous subsection, so in this one too this pattern of passion prediction, incomprehension, and instruction is followed by further scenes of both incomprehension and instruction (10:1-31). After a controversy with Pharisees over divorce, Jesus instructs the disciples that God forbids all divorce (10:2-12). Then, Jesus clashes several times with the disciples themselves. In these clashes, a fixed pattern emerges: Whereas the disciples repeatedly attest to their incomprehension by "thinking the things of humans," Jesus attests to his knowledge of the ways and will of God by "thinking the things of God."

For example, in turning away children brought to Jesus to be touched by him, the disciples reveal that in their view the people who count are not, like children, the unprivileged but persons of status and power (10:13);[32] for his part, Jesus receives the children and blesses them (10:14-16). Because the disciples also share the common belief that wealth is a sign of God's favor, they are aghast when Jesus asserts that a camel has a greater chance of passing through the eye of a needle than a rich person has of entering the kingdom of God (10:23-26). Shocked by this statement, the disciples pursue it: If it is impossible for even the rich to be saved, who then can be? Replies Jesus: Salvation lies beyond the control of all humans, for to bestow salvation is the prerogative of God (10:26-27). Finally, stirred to no little self-concern by Jesus' remarks, Peter wants Jesus to tell the disciples, who have left everything to follow him, what exactly the future has in store for them (10:28). Jesus' answer is that the first will be last and the last first: In this age, the disciples become members of a new community, but one that must endure persecution; in the age to come, they will inherit eternal life (10:29-31).

Jesus' Third Passion Prediction. Mark's third use of the pattern of passion prediction, incomprehension, and instruction occurs in the subsection 10:32-45. Still on the way to Jerusalem, Jesus yet again predicts his passion (10:32-34). Virtually point for point, he cites the major events that subsequently take place in the passion account itself (chaps. 14–16). For a third time, however, the disciples comprehend neither that Jesus' prediction describes the essence of his ministry—serving unto death—nor that what he says of his ministry has any relevancy for the way they are to perceive discipleship.

The disciples' incomprehension is epitomized by James and John (10:35-41). Even as Jesus speaks of giving his life, they wait to approach him to ask a favor. Because they view things from a human standpoint, they construe Jesus' journey to Jerusalem as a journey into the glory of God's end-time kingdom. The favor they ask is that Jesus grant them, once he takes his place in glory, the positions of greatest honor. Plainly, the agenda of James and John is not servanthood but self-aggrandizement. Also, when the ten become indignant over the brothers' request, they do so only because they covet the same positions for themselves.

Summoning the disciples, Jesus minces no words in instructing them on "thinking the things of God" about discipleship (10:42-45). In desiring for themselves positions of greatest honor, the disciples, Jesus declares, are operating the way gentile rulers do. Gentile rulers aspire to lord it over others, that is, to amass power so as to be able to control and dominate others. The way of power, however, is not the way of God's rule and therefore neither the way of Jesus nor the way of disciples. Instead of emulating gentile rulers, the disciples are to emulate Jesus himself: Just as it is his purpose to serve and not be served, so it is the purpose of disciples to be servants of one another and "slaves" of all.

On this note, Mark rounds out his threefold use of the pattern of passion prediction, incomprehension, and instruction. Through the vehicle of this pattern, Jesus has struggled with the disciples "on the way" from the regions of Caesarea Philippi to Jericho, only miles from Jerusalem.[33] As Jesus completes his journey to Jerusalem and enters the city, the disciples join the throng in hailing him as David's greater son (11:1-10). During his stay in Jerusalem, Jesus imparts further instruction to the disciples: He impresses upon them the power of faith (11:22-24) and stresses the need to forgive the neighbor if faith is not to become idle (11:25). He also holds up to them the example of the poor widow (12:43-44). In contrast to the scribes, whose feigned love of God is belied by their exploitation of the neighbor (12:38-40), the widow exemplifies complete love of God: In casting her "whole living" into the temple treasury, she in effect gives her "whole life" to God (12:44). Since the one event remaining before the beginning of the passion is Jesus' delivery of his eschatological discourse (chap. 13), the widow stands out as a fitting contrast also to the disciples: She demonstrates what it is "to think the things of God," whereas the disciples are yet beset with "thinking the things of humans."

Apostasy

In the passion account, the disciples are ironic figures: Because of their incomprehension, they badly misconstrue the true nature of things. Thinking themselves to be astute, courageous, and loyal, they are in reality imperceptive, cowardly, and faithless. Entering upon the passion, the disciples yet follow Jesus in commitment to him. As events unfold, however, they will renounce their commitment through word or deed and apostatize. As Jesus himself says of them: "The spirit indeed is willing, but the flesh is weak" (14:38).

Examples abound of the various ways in which the disciples' incomprehension finds expression in the passion account. Thus, if the reader is to regard the disciples as among those in the house of Simon the leper who wrongly become indignant,[34] then the disciples show in this scene already how blind they are to the true meaning of events (14:3-9). At Simon's house in Bethany, "some" there become angry when a woman comes up to Jesus and anoints his head with expensive nard ointment (14:3-5). As Jesus points out, however, what these persons judge to be a waste is in fact the anointing of his body in advance for burial (14:6-9). Again, when Judas goes to the chief priests and offers to betray Jesus (14:10-11), he has no inkling whatever that his treachery will abet God's plan of salvation (14:21). As Jesus predicts at the last supper that one of the twelve will betray him, one after another they all ask, "Is it I?" (14:17-19). In the mouths of both Judas and the eleven, their question is highly revealing. As formulated in the Greek, it anticipates a negative answer: "Surely it can't be I, can it?" As uttered by Judas, this question marks him out as a liar, for he asks it after having already sealed his pact with the chief priests (14:10-11). As uttered by the eleven, it attests to their enormous sense of false confidence: Each is certain he is incapable of betrayal. Yet again, when Jesus predicts at the Mount of Olives that all the disciples will forsake him and that Peter will deny him, Peter twice responds, both times with grand statements of ill-founded conviction (14:26-31). Peter first declares, "Even though all fall away, I will not!" (14:29). Next, he exclaims, "If I must die with you, I will not deny you!" (14:31). Adds Mark: "And they all [joined Peter and] said the same" (14:31). Finally, at Gethsemane Peter, James, and John graphically demonstrate how self-deluded the disciples really are: Having just pledged to die with Jesus rather than deny him, the three cannot muster the strength to watch with him even for an hour but instead fall asleep (14:33, 37, 40).

The end result of the disciples' incomprehension is apostasy, or defection: Judas betrays Jesus (14:43-46); all forsake him and flee (14:50); and Peter denies him (14:54, 66-72). Indeed, in denying Jesus, Peter, who had earlier vowed to die with Jesus, suddenly turns cowardly: Invoking a curse on himself, he swears, "I do not know this man of whom you speak" (14:66-72). With the betrayal, abandonment, and denial of Jesus, the disciples have severed their bonds of loyalty to him. Incomprehension has subverted commitment.

Reconciliation

The final mention of the disciples in Mark's story is by the angelic young man to the women at the empty tomb. "But go," he commands, "tell his disciples and Peter that he is going before you to Galilee; there you will see him, as he told you" (16:7). About the women, Mark himself comments in the final verse of his story: "And they went out and fled from the tomb . . . ; and they said nothing to any one, for they were afraid" (16:8).

The question the ending of Mark's story raises is whether Mark would have the reader construe his comment about the women's silence as frustrating the angel's command that they go and tell the disciples that Jesus will meet them in Galilee. If this question is answered in the affirmative, it means that the reader ends Mark's story understanding that the disciples forever remain alienated from Jesus: Because of the women's silence, the disciples are not told of the angel's command and hence never see Jesus in Galilee and never become his post-Easter apostles.[35] If this question is answered in the negative, it means that the reader ends Mark's story understanding that at some point the disciples are told of the angel's command so that they do go to Galilee and see Jesus and hence are to be thought of as having been reconciled to him.[36]

Mark invites the reader to think of the disciples as reconciled to Jesus following Easter. Within the world of Mark's story, Jesus is the Son of God, God's supreme agent who "thinks the things of God." Predictions and promises made by Jesus are reliable and certain. Obvious indications of this, for example, are the passion predictions, especially the third one, which is virtually a blueprint of events that later take place in the passion account itself (10:33-34). Important is the fact that in the same breath in which Jesus predicts the apostasy of the disciples, he also makes them a promise: "But after I am raised up, I will go before you to Galilee" (14:28). It is this promise of Jesus that the angel at the tomb explicitly takes up as he says to the women: "Go, tell his disciples and Peter that he is going before you to Galilee; there you will see him, as he told you" (16:7). Since in the world of Mark's story Jesus' word is firm and sure, the reader is invited to postulate that also Jesus' promise about seeing the disciples in Galilee comes to fulfillment. To be sure, Mark does not narrate a scene describing this fulfillment. Nevertheless, he obligates the reader to project it. As the reader projects the fulfillment of Jesus' promise, the reader in effect projects the resolution of Jesus' conflict with the disciples.

If Mark would have the reader project such fulfillment and resolution, what specifically is the reader to project? Apparently, the reader is to project three things, all of which have deep rootage in Mark's story.[37]

First, the reader should project that Jesus, in appearing to the disciples, reconciles them to himself. During his passion, Jesus predicted that God would smite the shepherd, that the sheep would be scattered, and that after he is raised, he would go before the disciples into Galilee (14:27-28). Subsequently, through Jesus' death the shepherd was smitten and the sheep, or disciples, were, through their defection, scattered. In seeing Jesus in Galilee following the resurrection, however, the scattered disciples are, through Jesus' word of promise, once again gathered to him. "Gathering the scattered" is a metaphor for reconciliation: Jesus gathers the scattered disciples, overcoming their alienation, and reconstitutes them as his followers.

Second, the reader should project that the disciples, in seeing Jesus, at last comprehend who he is and what he was about. At the transfiguration, the three disciples saw Jesus in heavenly splendor and were told by God himself that Jesus is his beloved Son (9:3, 7); Jesus, in turn, commanded the three to silence about this revelation until after the resurrection (9:9). In the parable of the wicked husbandmen, Jesus predicted death and resurrection for himself as the Son of God (12:6-8, 10-11). Against the background of these events, it becomes apparent that the disciples, seeing Jesus in Galilee following the resurrection, see him in heavenly splendor as the risen Son of God who nevertheless bears on his person the marks of the crucifixion. As the angel says of Jesus to the women, he is the one whom God has raised who, crucified in the past, still remains the crucified one (*ton estaurōmenon*, 16:6). Seeing Jesus as the risen yet crucified Son of God, the disciples finally comprehend what until now had eluded them: the secret of Jesus' identity as the Son of God and the purpose of his ministry, death on the cross (1:1; 9:7; 12:6-11; 15:39). As indicated at the transfiguration, the incomprehensible will, after the resurrection, become known (9:5-7, 9).

Third, the reader should project that the disciples, in seeing Jesus and comprehending who he is and what he was about, also comprehend that the essence of discipleship is servanthood. In the crucial section 8:27—10:45, Mark traces the failure of the disciples to comprehend that the essence of discipleship is servanthood to their failure to comprehend that servanthood is also the essence of Jesus' ministry. Because the disciples fail to comprehend Jesus' passion predictions concerning the heart of his ministry, so they also fail to comprehend his instructions on discipleship. In seeing Jesus in Galilee, however, the disciples do finally comprehend the truth of Jesus' passion predictions: They see Jesus as the crucified one whom God has nevertheless raised. Correspondingly, the disciples also now comprehend the instructions he earlier gave them on discipleship, for example: "If anyone would come after me, let him deny himself and take up his cross, and let him follow me" (8:34). The disciples understand that the essence of discipleship is servanthood.

Accordingly, the resolution of Jesus' conflict with the disciples in Mark's story is reconciliation, and the reader projects that the disciples do become Jesus' post-Easter apostles. It is in anticipation of this eventuality that Jesus delivers to (the four of) them his eschatological discourse (chap. 13). In this discourse, he predicts the events the disciples will encounter in the time between his resurrection and Parousia.

Summary

In the beginning of his story (1:1-13), Mark presents Jesus to the reader. After Jesus commences his ministry in the middle of the story (1:14—8:26), Mark introduces the disciples. In the first half of the middle, the picture that Mark sketches of the disciples is highly favorable. The emphasis is on the call of the disciples, the creation of the twelve, who epitomize Jesus' disciples, and the ministry of the twelve to Israel. Those chosen by Jesus to be his disciples give him their undivided loyalty and are called to be with him and to engage in mission. Enlightened by God about the secret of his end-time rule and empowered by Jesus for ministry in Israel, the disciples do as Jesus does: They preach, teach, heal, and exorcise demons.

In the latter half of the middle of his story, Mark depicts the disciples in unflattering colors. Although enlightened by God and empowered by Jesus, the disciples show themselves to be uncomprehending. In hearing Jesus' parables and in three boat scenes interspersed by two feeding miracles, the disciples comprehend neither Jesus' parables nor his identity nor the true nature of either his authority or the authority granted them. The upshot is that in situations calling for insight, trust, courage, confession, and action, the disciples fail miserably. At the root of their incomprehension is the way they view reality: Whereas Jesus views reality in the light of God's end-time rule and "thinks the things of God," the disciples view reality in human terms and "think the things of humans." Jesus' conflict with the disciples is to lead them to adopt his view of reality.

This conflict between Jesus and the disciples becomes critical in the end of Mark's story (8:27—16:8). The issue at stake is the meaning of Jesus' ministry and therefore also the meaning of discipleship (e.g., 8:31, 34-35). Three times Jesus predicts his passion, in so doing describing the essence of his ministry as servanthood ("submission to suffering and the taking of his life"). Three times the disciples indicate by what they say or do that they do not, and will not, comprehend Jesus' passion predictions. Three times Jesus also instructs the disciples that servanthood is likewise the essence of discipleship. Because the disciples do not comprehend what Jesus says of his own ministry, they similarly do not comprehend what he says of discipleship. Whereas Jesus "thinks the things of God," the disciples continue to "think the things of humans." Repeatedly, Jesus clashes with the disciples, for instead of hearing his summons to be servant and slave of all, the disciples are desirous of status, greatness, the blessings of wealth, positions of power, a secure future, and a life without suffering.

Where the disciples' incomprehension leads them Mark makes clear in the passion account (chaps. 14–16). Though committed to Jesus, the disciples are unable to perceive aright either themselves or the events in which they are enmeshed. Though willing in spirit, they are weak in flesh (14:38). As a result, the disciples are unable to remain loyal to Jesus and commit apostasy: Judas betrays him, all forsake him, and Peter denies him. In the passion account, incomprehension subverts commitment.

This notwithstanding, Mark invites the reader at the end of his story to project yet a final impression of the disciples.

The validity of this impression rests on the belief Mark has urged on the reader that Jesus' word is reliable and certain. During his passion, Jesus promised the disciples that after he is raised, he would go before them into Galilee, where, the angel adds, they will see him (14:28; 16:7). To project the disciples as seeing Jesus in Galilee following Easter is to project at least three things, to wit: (*a*) that Jesus gathers the scattered disciples and therefore reconciles them to himself; (*b*) that the disciples, seeing Jesus as the risen yet crucified Son of God, at last comprehend both the secret of his identity and the purpose of his ministry; and (*c*) that comprehending the essence of Jesus' ministry, the disciples also comprehend that servanthood is the essence of discipleship. Accordingly, the resolution of Jesus' conflict with the disciples in Mark's story is not, finally, alienation but reconciliation. Reconciled to Jesus and viewing reality from his standpoint, the disciples move toward the future as Jesus described this for them in his eschatological discourse of chapter 13.

Abbreviations

AnBib	Analecta biblica
2 Apoc. Bar.	*Syriac Apocalypse of Baruch*
BKAT	Biblischer Kommentar: Altes Testament
BLS	Bible and Literature Series
BR	*Biblical Research*
CBQ	*Catholic Biblical Quarterly*
CBQMS	Catholic Biblical Quarterly—Monograph Series
CEP	Contemporary Evangelical Perspectives
CGTC	Cambridge Greek Testament Commentaries
CRINT	Compendia rerum iudaicarum ad novum testamentum
EKK	Evangelisch-katholischer Kommentar zum Neuen Testament
1 Enoch	*Ethiopic Enoch*
GBS	Guides to Biblical Scholarship
HTKNT	Herders theologischer Kommentar zum Neuen Testament
IDB	G. A. Buttrick, ed., *Interpreter's Dictionary of the Bible*
IDBSup	Supplementary volume to *IDB*
Int	*Interpretation*
JBL	*Journal of Biblical Literature*
JR	*Journal of Religion*
JSNTSup	Journal for the Study of New Testament—Supplement Series
LXX	Septuagint
NovTSup	Supplements to Novum Testamentum

NT	New Testament
NTL	New Testament Library
NTS	*New Testament Studies*
NVBS	New Voices in Biblical Studies
OT	Old Testament
PC	Proclamation Commentaries
PGC	Pelican Gospel Commentaries
RSR	*Recherches de science religieuse*
SAJ	Studies in Ancient Judaism
SBLDS	SBL Dissertation Series
SBS	Stuttgarter Bibelstudien
SNTW	Studies of the New Testament and Its World
ST	*Studia theologica*
TDNT	G. Kittel and G. Friedrich, eds., *Theological Dictionary of the New Testament* (Grand Rapids: Wm. B. Eerdmans, 1964–76)
TI	Theological Inquiries
ZNW	*Zeitschrift für die neutestamentliche Wissenschaft*

Notes

(Works referred to more than once or listed in the Selected Bibliography are cited by author's last name and title only).

1. Introduction

1. On Jewish apocalyptic literature, see J. J. Collins, *The Apocalyptic Imagination: An Introduction to the Jewish Matrix of Christianity* (New York: Crossroad, 1984).

2. M. H. Abrams, *A Glossary of Literary Terms* (4th ed.; New York: Holt, Rinehart & Winston, 1981), 175.

3. The most extensive treatment to date of the "spatial settings" in Mark's story (e.g., "Galilee," "Judea," "the way," "sea," "mountain," "synagogue," "house") is that of Malbon, *Narrative Space and Mythic Meaning*. For a survey of Markan settings, see Rhoads and Michie, *Mark as Story*, 63-72.

4. See, e.g., Mark 1:16, 18, 21, 23, 29, 40; 2:1, 13, 14, 15.

5. For a discussion of the "Jewish homeland" vs. "foreign lands" in Mark's story, see Malbon, *Narrative Space and Mythic Meaning*, 40-44.

6. Ibid., 72-75. See Mark 1:2-6, 12-13.

7. Ibid., 44-46.

8. See Mark 14:28; 16:7.

9. On "Jerusalem" and its environs, see Malbon, *Narrative Space and Mythic Meaning*, 46-49.

10. See Mark 3:22; 7:1; 10:32, 33-34.

11. On the "temple," see Malbon, *Narrative Space and Mythic Meaning*, 137-39.

121

12. A "major character" is a figure like Jesus or an identifiable group like the disciples who appears throughout the greater part of Mark's story. On this view, figures like John the Baptist, Herod Antipas, and Pilate, significant though they may be, are nonetheless not major characters. For a slightly different count, see Rhoads and Michie, *Mark as Story*, 101.

13. On God's "point of view" as normative in Mark's story, see Kingsbury, *Christology of Mark's Gospel*, 47-50. For a highly instructive, general treatment of the topic "point of view" in Mark, see N. Petersen, " 'Point of View' in Mark's Narrative," *Semeia* 12 (1978): 97-121.

14. Mark 12:6; see also 14:36.

15. Mark 12:6; see also 1:14-15; 4:26-29, 30-32.

16. Mark 12:9; see also 13:10; 14:9.

17. Mark 12:9-11; see also 1:17; 3:35; 10:29-30; 14:28; 16:7.

18. See Mark 3:11-12; also 1:24-25, 34; 5:7.

19. For information on this term, see, e.g., T. H. Gaster, "Beelzebul," *IDB* 1:374.

20. See Mark 15:1, 9, 12, 18, 26.

21. So also W. A. Kort, *Story, Text, and Scripture: Literary Interests in Biblical Narrative* (University Park, Pa.: Pennsylvania State University Press, 1988), 46-47.

22. This point is aptly made by Rhoads and Michie, *Mark as Story*, 105-8.

23. See, e.g., Mark 1:38-39; 3:31-35; 10:21, 42-45.

24. So also Rhoads and Michie, *Mark as Story*, 108.

25. Cf., e.g., Mark 8:34-35 with 15:24-37.

26. See, e.g., Mark 1:17-18, 20; 2:14; 3:13-16; 10:28.

27. See, e.g., Mark 4:13; 7:18; 8:17-21, 33; 9:19; [14:6].

28. Cf. Mark 14:18, 27, 30 with 14:28; 16:7.

29. See, e.g., Mark 1:40-42; 9:21-27.

30. On the attitude of the authorities toward John, cf., e.g., Mark 1:4-5 with 11:30-31. On their attitude toward Jesus, cf., e.g., Mark 1:14-15 with 3:22, 30.

31. See Mark 2:15-16, 18, 23; 3:7, 9.

32. See Mark 1:16, 19, 29; 3:17; 10:35, 41.

33. See Mark 5:37; 9:2; 14:33.

34. See Mark 1:30, 36; 8:29, 32, 33; 9:5; 10:28; 11:21; 14:29, 37, 54, 66-72; 16:7.

35. See Mark 14:10-11, 43-45.

36. See Mark 3:19; 14:10-11, 18-21, 43-45.

37. On Peter as spokesman for the disciples, see Mark 8:29-30, 32-33; 9:5-6; 10:28; 14:31, 37-38. On Peter as being typical of the disciples, cf. Mark 1:16-18 with 10:28; 8:29-30; 14:29 with 14:50; 14:31 with 14:54, 66-72.

38. On the disciples as "loyal," see also Rhoads and Michie, *Mark as Story*, 124. In contrast to my position, however, the latter do not regard "being loyal" as a "root character trait" from which others spring.

39. See Mark 1:16-20; 3:13-16; 10:28.

40. Thus, Jesus imparts to the disciples authority (3:15; 6:7) and they, in turn, preach (3:14; 6:12), teach (6:30), heal (6:13), and cast out demons (3:15; 6:13). In returning to him, they report all they have done and taught (6:30).

41. Cf., e.g., Mark 1:38; 3:9 with 4:1 and 4:35-36; 3:13; 6:7-8 with 6:12-13; 6:31-32, 38, 41, 45; 8:1, 6-7.

42. See Mark 2:15-16, 18, 23-24; 7:1-5.

43. See esp. Mark 2:18-20; 7:1-2, 5; also 2:15, 23-28.

44. See Mark 3:15; 6:7.

45. Within the story world of Mark, the Herodians appear to be thought of as agents of Herod Antipas (cf. 3:6 and 12:13 with 8:15) who nonetheless function in effect as "religious authorities" because of their close association with the Pharisees. With the Pharisees, the Herodians both plot Jesus' death (3:6) and engage him in debate (12:13-17).

46. In determining the character portrait that Mark sketches of the religious authorities, one does best not to make use of the figure of Joseph of Arimathea. Mark describes Joseph as a "prominent counselor" (15:43). Does this mean that he is to be regarded as a member of the Sanhedrin (see R. E. Brown, "The Burial of Jesus [Mark 15:42-47]," *CBQ* 50 [1988]: 239)? Many scholars believe that Mark himself forecloses this possibility, since he states that "all" the members of the Sanhedrin condemned Jesus to death (14:64; also 15:1; see Matera, *Kingship of Jesus*, 55). These scholars reason that Joseph is rather to be thought of as a member of a local, or provincial, council (so, e.g., J. Gnilka, *Das Evangelium nach Markus* [EKK 2; Zürich and Neukirchen-Vluyn: Benziger Verlag and Neukirchener Verlag, 1979] 2.332). However this may be, what is decisive literary-critically is that the role Joseph plays within the story-world of Mark is analogous to that of Jairus, who is a "leader [president] of a synagogue" (5:22). Just as Jairus belongs to that circle of minor characters who exhibit great faith in Jesus' power to heal, so Joseph

belongs to that circle of minor characters who, in contrast to the disciples, exemplify what it means to "serve."

47. See, e.g., Mark 12:1; 14:1-2; 15:1.

48. This understanding of "hypocrisy" comes to light in the passages in which Mark uses either this term or the cognate "hypocrite" (see Mark 7:6-7; 12:14-15; also 12:38-40).

49. Jesus bluntly tells the Sadducees that they err (12:24, 27), and what he says of them can easily be seen to apply to the other religious authorities as well.

50. See Mark 2:25-26; 12:10-11, 26-27.

51. On the meaning of Mark 12:35-37, see Kingsbury, *Christology of Mark's Gospel*, 108-14.

52. When Mark has the "friendly scribe" say that "love of God and neighbor" are to take precedence over "all whole burnt offerings and sacrifices" (12:32-33), Mark is in effect using the friendly scribe to identify the two contrasting positions of Jesus and the authorities on doing the will of God. As we noted, doing God's will is, for Jesus, exercising love. For the religious authorities, it is attending to the letter of law and tradition as defined by them. Correctly but somewhat grandly, Rhoads and Michie (*Mark as Story*, 120) designate love of God and neighbor as "Jesus' constitutional principle of legal interpretation."

53. See Mark 3:22.

54. See Mark 2:23-28; 3:1-5.

55. See Mark 2:15-17, [18-20]; 7:1-13.

56. See Mark 11:15-18; also 14:56-58.

57. See Mark 11:15-18; 12:1-12 (esp. v. 9).

58. See Mark 3:6; 11:18.

59. See Mark 12:12.

60. See Mark 14:1.

61. See Mark 11:18; 12:12; 14:1-2.

62. See Mark 12:37; 14:43, 48-49.

63. See Mark 1:28, 39, 45; 6:14.

64. See Mark 1:45; 2:13; 3:7-8; 10:1.

65. See Mark 2:2; 3:20; 4:1; 5:21; also 8:1.

66. See Mark 3:7; 5:24; 10:46.

67. See Mark 3:9; 5:24, 31; also 4:1.

68. See Mark 3:20; 6:31.

69. See Mark 3:9; 4:36; 6:31-32, 45; 7:17; [8:9-10].

70. See Mark 2:2; [4:33].

71. See Mark 8:34; also 3:32-35.

72. See Mark 3:32-35; 4:10; 15:41.
73. See Mark 2:13; 4:1-2; 6:6, 34; 10:1; 14:49.
74. See Mark 1:21-22; 6:2; 11:18; 12:37.
75. See Mark 1:34; 3:10-12; 6:6, 53-56.
76. See Mark 1:27; 6:2.
77. See Mark 3:10; 6:56; also 5:28.
78. See Mark 6:35-44; 8:1-9 (v. 21).
79. See Mark 6:14-15; 8:27-28.
80. See Mark 6:51-52.
81. See Mark 14:43, 48-49.
82. In their treatment of characterization in Mark's story, Rhoads and Michie (*Mark as Story*, 129-34) provide an exemplary discussion of the minor characters under the category of "the little people." See further, J. Dewey, *Disciples of the Way: Mark on Discipleship* (Women's Division, Board of Global Ministries, The United Methodist Church, 1976), chap. 6.
83. On this point, see also Rhoads and Michie, *Mark as Story*, 130.
84. Arguably, one might add to this list two other examples: those who bring the deaf and speech-impaired man to Jesus for healing (7:32-37); and those who bring the blind man to Jesus to be touched by him (8:22-26).
85. See Mark 9:33-37; 10:13-16.
86. This point is well noted by Rhoads and Michie, *Mark as Story*, 132-33.
87. Joseph of Arimathea is described by Mark as a "prominent counselor" (15:43). By itself, this description suggests that Joseph is to be regarded as a member either of the Sanhedrin or, what many scholars think more likely, of a local, or provincial, council. Still, in terms of the role Joseph plays in Mark's story, his place as a character is manifestly not with the religious authorities but, as here, with those minor characters who show what it is to "serve." See above, n. 46.
88. For a succinct and insightful discussion of plot, see F. J. Matera, "The Plot of Matthew's Gospel," *CBQ* 49 (1987): 235-40.
89. On the importance of the element of conflict in Mark's story, see Rhoads and Michie, *Mark as Story*, 73-77.

2. The Story of Jesus

1. This chapter is informed by my own study of Mark's portrait of Jesus (Kingsbury, *Christology of Mark's Gospel*, chaps. 3–4). For

other, in part, contrasting views of Mark's Christology, see, e.g., Donahue, *Are You the Christ?;* Perrin, *Pilgrimage in New Testament Christology;* Achtemeier, *Mark,* chap. 6; Petersen, *Literary Criticism,* 60-68; R. C. Tannehill, "The Gospel of Mark as Narrative Christology," *Semeia* 16 (1979): 57-95; Matera, *Kingship of Jesus,* chaps. 5–7; Boring, *Truly Human/Truly Divine;* and Robbins, *Jesus the Teacher.* For a recent survey of scholarly research on Mark's Christology, see Matera, *What Are They Saying About Mark?,* chap. 2.

2. But see, e.g., 1:4-6; 6:17-29.

3. Scholars construe the first verse of Mark's Gospel in one of three ways: (*a*) Most understand it, as I do also, as the "title" to the whole of Mark's gospel story (see, e.g., V. Taylor, *The Gospel According to St. Mark* [London: Macmillan Co., 1959], 152). (*b*) Others see it as relating to the section 1:1-13 (see, e.g., C. E. B. Cranfield, *The Gospel According to St. Mark* [CGTC; Cambridge: Cambridge University Press, 1959], 34-35). And (*c*) still others see it as relating to the section 1:1-15 (see, e.g., R. A. Guelich, " 'The Beginning of the Gospel': Mark 1:1-15," *BR* 27 [1982]: 8). Considering the data, one can develop a strong rationale for each of the three options.

4. See Mark 13:10; 14:9.

5. See, e.g., Mark 1:14-15; 8:34-35; 13:10; 14:24; 15:38.

6. Although Mark designates John as "John the Baptizer" (see 1:4; 6:14, 24), he also designates him as "John the Baptist" (see 6:25; 8:28). For the sake of convenience, I shall consistently designate John as "John the Baptist."

7. See Isa. 40:1-11.

8. Cf. Mark 1:4 with 1:14-15.

9. Cf. Mark 2:18; 6:29 with 1:16-20; 3:13-19.

10. Cf. Mark 1:5 with 3:7-9.

11. Cf., e.g., Mark 1:7-8 with 8:31; 9:31; 10:33-34; chap. 13.

12. Cf. Mark 11:31 with 12:1-12; 14:63-64.

13. Cf. Mark 1:14 with 14:43-46.

14. Cf. Mark 6:14-29 with 15:1-15.

15. This "son of God" in Psalm 2, however, is a young man from the line of David who is in the process of becoming king of Judah. During the service of his coronation, the prophet utters the words "My son are you" on behalf of God, and thus the king-designate is adopted by God as his son (see H. J. Kraus, *Psalmen* [BKAT 15; Neukirchen-Vluyn: Neukirchener Verlag], 1:18-19). In Mark's story, by contrast, the idea is not that God adopts Jesus as his Son in

the act of declaring who he is but that God states what is already the case: Jesus *is* his Son.

16. On God's "point of view" as being normative in Mark's story, see Kingsbury, *Christology of Mark's Gospel*, 47-50.

17. See, e.g., Isa. 11:6-9; 65:25; *2 Apoc. Bar.* 73:6.

18. The principal activities in which Jesus engages during his public ministry in and around Galilee are highlighted by Mark in the first three summary passages he places in the middle of his story: 1:14-15 (preaching); 1:21-22 (teaching); and 1:32-34 (healing and exorcising demons). In addition, see 1:16-20 (calling disciples).

19. See Mark 1:16-20; 2:14; 3:13-19.

20. See further, Mark 2:13; 4:1-9, 26-34; 6:2, 6b, 34; 7:1-23; also 10:1; 11:17-18; 12:14, 35; 14:49.

21. See Mark 1:32-34; 3:7-12; 6:53-56.

22. See Mark 1:32-34, 39; 3:27.

23. See, e.g., Mark 1:21-22, 27; 2:12; 5:42; 6:2, 51; 7:37; also 9:15; 10:24, 26; 11:18; 12:17.

24. See, e.g., Mark 1:32-33, 37, 45; 2:1-2, 13; 3:7-8, 20, 32; 4:1-2; 5:21, 27; 6:32-34, 53-56; 7:24; 8:1-2.

25. See Mark 2:15; 3:7; 5:24.

26. See, e.g., Mark 1:45; 3:9-10, 20; 4:35-36; 5:24, 31; 6:31-32, 45-46.

27. See also Mark 1:24, 34; 5:7.

28. See Mark 1:25, 34; 3:12.

29. On this point, see Kingsbury, *Christology of Mark's Gospel*, 86-88.

30. See ibid. The specific contrapuntal pattern is this: demonic cry (1:24), question (1:27), demonic cries (1:34), question (2:7), demonic cries (3:11), question (4:41), demonic cry (5:7), question (6:3).

31. For a concise discussion of the motif of "on the way," see Malbon, *Mythic Meaning and Narrative Space*, 68-71.

32. See Mark 1:16-20; 2:7; 3:13-19.

33. Thus, the disciples too, on the divine authority Jesus himself gave them (3:14-16; 6:7, 12-13, 30), have preached (3:15; 6:12), taught (6:30), healed (6:13), and exorcised demons (3:15; 6:7, 13).

34. See Mark 1:1, 11; 9:7.

35. On the Markan chronology spanning the section 11:1—16:8, see F. J. Matera (*Passion Narratives and Gospel Theologies: Interpreting the Synoptics Through Their Passion Stories* [TI; New York: Paulist Press, 1986], 12-13), who acknowledges his indebtedness to R. Pesch

(*Das Markusevangelium* [HTKNT 2; Freiburg: Herder, 1977], 2:323-28); see also Gnilka, *Evangelium nach Markus*, 2:220, esp. n. 8.

36. In Mark's story, to grasp something with the mind and to reject it with the heart is what may be termed "obdurate understanding." On this, see M. Boucher, *Mysterious Parable: A Literary Study* (CBQMS 6; Washington, D.C.: Catholic Biblical Association of America, 1977), 83-84.

37. See Mark 1:11; 9:7.

38. See 12:35-37, 38-40 (note v. 37b).

39. See Mark 12:41-44; chap. 13. Also G. Stählin, "*Chēra*," *TDNT* 9 (1974): 449.

40. For further reading on the passion account, consult the following: Achtemeier, *Mark*, chap. 10; Kelber, ed., *Passion in Mark*; Petersen, *Literary Criticism*, 73-78; Senior, *Passion of Jesus*; Matera, *Kingship of Jesus*; idem, *Passion Narratives*; Robbins, *Jesus the Teacher*, 180-96.

41. See Matera (*Passion Narratives*, 13), who follows, with slight variation, Pesch (*Markusevangelium*, 2:323). According to Pesch's scheme, Jesus' entry into Jerusalem takes places on Sunday (11:1-11). On Monday, Jesus curses the fig tree and cleanses the temple (11:12-19). On Tuesday, Jesus teaches in the temple and delivers his eschatological discourse (11:20—13:37). On Wednesday, the first events of the passion narrative take place (14:1-11). On Thursday, Jesus sends two disciples to make preparations for the eating of the Passover (14:12-16). (On Thursday evening, Jesus celebrates his last meal with the disciples and is arrested [14:17-72].) On Friday, Jesus is crucified (15:1-47). Saturday is the sabbath day, referred to retrospectively at 16:1. And on Sunday, the women journey to the tomb (16:2). See further, Gnilka, *Evangelium nach Markus*, 2:220 n. 8. It should be noted that in contrast to these three scholars, Achtemeier (*Mark*, 97-98) expresses skepticism as to whether any "last week" in Jesus' life can indeed be discerned in Mark's narrative.

42. In line with 2 Chron. 35:17, it appears that Mark regards the Passover festival and the Feast of Unleavened Bread as being synonymous.

43. Literally, Mark 14:1 reads that "after two days" it was the Passover and the Feast of Unleavened Bread. D. E. Nineham (*The Gospel of St Mark* [PGC; New York: Seabury Press, 1968], 373) speaks for numerous scholars when he notes that the expression detailing two days "may mean that the Passover would occur forty-eight hours later, or, if the reckoning is inclusive, that it would occur the next

day." In regard to the time scheme he finds governing Mark's passion account, Pesch (see above, n. 41) reckons with two days, not one, by working back from Friday (but see Pesch's comments on 14:12). By contrast, Matera (*Passion Narratives*, 12-13) reckons with one day, not two, apparently by counting forward from Tuesday. Both Pesch and Matera agree, however, that Wednesday is the day on which the first events of the passion narrative take place (14:1-11), and this position is supported by both Gnilka (*Evangelium nach Markus*, 2:220) and Senior (*Passion of Jesus*, 43).

44. In determining the time scheme of the last week in Jesus' life, Pesch (see above, n. 41) assumes the Jewish mode of reckoning days (from sunset to sunset), whereas Gnilka (*Evangelium nach Markus*, 2:219-20) works with the Greco-Roman mode (from midnight to midnight). For Gnilka, therefore, "Thursday evening" is still part of Thursday, but for Pesch it is the beginning hours of Friday.

45. See above, n. 41 (also Matera, *Passion Narratives*, 13). The reference to the "day of Preparation, that is, the day before the sabbath," at 15:42 shows that Mark intends to identify Friday as the day of Jesus' death (see Taylor, *St. Mark*, 599; and Nineham, *St Mark*, 434).

46. See, e.g., Mark 15:1, 25, 33, 34, 42.

47. See Mark 14:10, 55; 15:1, 10, 11, 31; observe also the references to the high priest: Mark 14:47, 53, 54, 60, 61, 63, 66. At the time of Jesus, the high priest was the head of the chief priests and the presiding officer of the Sanhedrin. Apart from the high priest, the Sanhedrin, or High Council, numbered seventy persons and was made up of three groups: the chief priests, the scribes, and the elders. The chief priests were a group of about ten wealthy priests (alternately, three or four prominent laymen could also be found among them) who supervised the temple and sacrificial system at Jerusalem. The scribes were experts at interpreting the law; they were the theologians and jurists of the day. And the elders were wealthy patricians representing leading aristocratic families. The Sanhedrin functioned, in effect, as the domestic government of the Jews, as a type of senate, or parliament, with executive, legislative, and judicial authority. Tax affairs and military authority, however, reposed in the hands of the Roman prefect. Whereas scribes apparently belonged to the party of either the Pharisees or the Sadducees, the chief priests and the elders belonged to the party of the Sadducees. For a detailed discussion of the preceding, see

B. Reicke, *The New Testament Era* (Philadelphia: Fortress Press, 1968), 138-63.

48. See Mark 14:43-52; 14:53—15:39.

49. Within the world of Mark's story, it is Jesus' claim to be the Son of the Blessed [God] that provokes the high priest to charge him with blasphemy, not his assertion that he is "the man" whom they "will see . . . sitting at the right hand of Power [God] and coming with the clouds of heaven" (14:62). The correctness of this observation is apparent from 8:38. Here Jesus makes a claim similar to that of 14:62b, tacitly referring to himself in public (8:34) as "the man" who will "come in the glory of his Father with the holy angels," yet this claim elicits no response of condemnation.

50. See, e.g., H. W. Beyer, *"Blasphēmeō," TDNT* 1 (1964): 622-23.

51. On the theme of Jesus as the "righteous sufferer," see Matera, *Passion Narratives*, 39-48.

52. See Mark 12:29-30.

53. See B. Gerhardsson, "Du judéo-christianisme à Jésus par le Shema," *RSR* 60 (1972): 29.

54. See ibid., 29-30.

55. See Mark 13:2; 14:58; 15:29; also Donahue, *Are You the Christ?* 201-3; Senior, *Passion of Jesus*, 126-29. On the question of which temple curtain is meant (the "outer one" shielding the entrance to the holy place or the "inner one" covering the holy of holies), scholars continue to be of two minds. Whereas Donahue, for example, argues for the outer one, Senior argues for the inner one. For a discussion of the temple of Herod, see W. F. Stinespring, "Temple, Jerusalem," *IDB* 4:550-60; and M. Ben-Dov, "Temple of Herod," IDBSup, 870-72.

56. On this view of Jesus' death in Mark's story, see A. J. Hultgren, *Christ and His Benefits: Christology and Redemption in the New Testament* (Philadelphia: Fortress Press, 1987), 61-64; also Gnilka, *Evangelium nach Markus*, 2:245-46; and Pesch, *Markusevangelium*, 2:358-60.

57. For a discussion of the last supper against the background of other parts of Mark's story, see Senior, *Passion of Jesus*, 53-62.

58. The notion that the risen Jesus is one with the crucified Jesus is also grounded in Mark 12:10-11. In the OT, a play on words occurs according to which the term "stone" becomes a metaphor for "son" (see 1 Kings 18:31; Isa. 54:11-13; Lam. 4:1-2; and M. Black, "The Christological Use of the Old Testament in the New Testament," *NTS* 18 [1971/72]: 1-14). This play on words seems to lie at the basis of Mark's use of Ps. 118:22-23 at 12:10-11: The

"stone" rejected by the builders which the Lord places at the head of the corner refers to the "Son" crucified by Israel whom God will raise from the dead and thus vindicate.

59. See Mark 14:62; also 8:38—9:1; 13:24-27.

60. See Mark 13:24-27; 14:62.

61. See Mark 2:10, 28; 8:31, 38; 9:9, 12, 31; 10:33, 45; 13:26; 14:21, 41, 62.

62. For a more detailed discussion of "the Son of man" in Mark's story, see Kingsbury, *Christology of Mark's Gospel*, chap. 4.

63. See further Mark 8:34, 38.

3. The Story of the Authorities

1. Two redaction-critical studies of some or all of these groups are: M. C. Cook, *Mark's Treatment of the Jewish Leaders* (NovTSup 51; Leiden: E. J. Brill, 1978); and D. Lührmann, "Die Pharisäer und die Schriftgelehrten im Markusevangelium," *ZNW* 78 (1987): 169-85. Both of these studies are interested in answering the historical question of how familiar the evangelist Mark himself was with Jewish leadership groups. Whereas Cook concludes that the only leadership group of whom the evangelist may have had first-hand knowledge is the Pharisees (p. 28), Lührmann contends that the evangelist's presentation of the leaders shows that his community was embroiled in actual conflict with Jewish scribes but not with any of the other groups, not even Pharisees (pp. 183-85).

2. For a historical overview of the respective groups of religious authorities, see Reicke, *New Testament Era*, 141-68.

3. For two, quite different, historical assessments of the Pharisees, see J. Neusner, *From Politics to Piety: The Emergence of Pharisaic Judaism* (2d ed.; New York: Ktav, 1979); and E. Rivkin, *A Hidden Revolution: The Pharisees' Search for the Kingdom Within* (Nashville: Abingdon Press, 1978).

4. It should be noted, however, that this view, widely held by scholars, is vigorously disputed by J. Neusner (see, e.g., *The Pharisees: Rabbinic Perspectives* [SAJ; Hoboken, N.J.: Ktav, 1973], 230-32). Neusner contends that while the Pharisees at the time of Jesus certainly possessed traditions, they had no "tradition of the elders" that they cultivated as oral law and regarded as an extension of the written law of Moses.

5. See, however, n. 4.

6. See, e.g., Mark 14:53, 55.

7. During the prefecture of A.D. 6–41, the Sanhedrin served as the domestic government of Judea (= Idumea, Judea, and Samaria). During the procuratorship of A.D. 44–66, its power extended also to Galilee. See Reicke, *New Testament Era*, 134, 144; also M. Stern, "The Province of Judaea," in *The Jewish People in the First Century*, ed. S. Safrai and M. Stern (CRINT 1/1; Philadelphia: Fortress Press, 1974), chap. 6.

8. For two assessments of the historical evidence on the Herodians, see A. J. Hultgren, *Jesus and His Adversaries: The Form and Function of the Conflict Stories in the Synoptic Tradition* (Minneapolis: Augsburg Publishing House, 1979), 154-56; and S. Sandmel, "Herodians," *IDB* 2:594-95.

9. See, e.g., Mark 11:18; 14:1, 10-11; 55; 15:1, 10, 11, 31.

10. For a form- and redaction-critical study of the controversies Jesus has with the religious authorities as found in Mark, Matthew, and Luke, see Hultgren, *Jesus and His Adversaries*.

11. See, e.g., Mark 4:38; 9:17, 38; 10:17, 20, 35; 12:14, 19, 32; 13:1; also 9:5; 10:51; 11:21; 14:45.

12. See also Rhoads and Michie, *Mark as Story*, 86. In her study of 2:1—3:6, Dewey (*Markan Public Debate*, 116) calls attention to the trend in this section toward a heightening of conflict but sees it as developing along different lines.

13. See, e.g., Taylor, *St. Mark*, 365.

14. For a careful and illuminating study of this cycle of debates, see Dewey, *Markan Public Debate*.

15. In illustration of this kind of thinking, see, e.g., Luke 13:3-5; John 9:1-2, 34.

16. See, e.g., Exod. 34:6-7; Pss. 103:2-3; 130:3-4; Isa. 43:25; Dan. 9:9. Also Beyer, *"Blasphēmeō,"* 623.

17. See, e.g., Neusner, *From Politics to Piety*, 67, 80.

18. Ibid.

19. See, e.g., Reicke, *New Testament Era*, 139; and O. Michel, *"Telonēs,"* *TDNT* 8 (1972): 101-3.

20. See K. H. Rengstorf, *"Hamartōlos,"* *TDNT* 1 (1964): 327.

21. See, e.g., N. Perrin, *Rediscovering the Teaching of Jesus* (NTL; London: SCM Press, 1967), 102-8.

22. See, e.g., J. Behm, *"Nēstis,"* *TDNT* 4 (1967): 927-33.

23. This view is well expressed by Nineham (*St Mark*, 105).

24. Mark's quotation of Isaiah in 7:6-7 stems from the Septuagint (LXX), the Greek translation of the Hebrew OT.

25. See O. Linton, "The Demand for a Sign from Heaven," *ST* 19 (1965): 112-29.

26. For an explanation of the various details Mark cites in 11:15-16, see Taylor, *St. Mark*, 462-63.

27. On this point, see the discussion by Matera, *Passion Narratives*, 67-68.

28. On the tearing of the temple curtain, see the literature and remarks found above in chapter 2, n. 55.

29. See, e.g., Nineham, *St Mark*, 316.

30. On the view of the resurrected life as being comparable to the existence angels enjoy, see *1 Enoch* 104:2, 4 (also 15:6-7; 62:14-16); *2 Apoc. Bar.* 51:8-10.

31. See, e.g., 2 Chron. 35:17.

32. On the meaning of the phrase "after two days" in Mark 14:1, see above, chapter 2, n. 43.

33. On the chronology of Mark's passion, see above, chapter 2, n. 41.

34. See Mark 8:31; 9:31; 10:33-34.

35. See, e.g., Mark 8:38; 9:1; 12:10-11, 36; 13:26-27; 14:62.

4. The Story of the Disciples

1. Specialized studies on the disciples in Mark abound. I mention the following because they represent a good cross section of both methods of study and views: R. P. Meye, *Jesus and the Twelve: Discipleship and Revelation in Mark's Gospel* (Grand Rapids: Wm. B. Eerdmans, 1968); K.-G. Reploh, *Markus—Lehrer der Gemeinde: Eine redaktionsgeschichtliche Studie zu den Jüngerperikopen des Markus-Evangeliums* (SBS 9; Stuttgart: Verlag Katholisches Bibelwerk, 1969); R. E. Brown, K. P. Donfried, and J. Reumann, *Peter in the New Testament* (Minneapolis and New York: Augsburg Publishing House and Paulist Press, 1973), chap. 5; Achtemeir, *Mark*, chap. 11; K. Stock, *Boten aus dem Mit-Ihm Sein: Das Verhältnis zwischen Jesus und den Zwölf nach Markus* (AnBib 70; Rome: Biblical Institute Press, 1975); Dewey, *Disciples on the Way;* R. C. Tannehill, "The Disciples in Mark: The Function of a Narrative Role," *JR* 57 (1977): 386-405; Best, *Following Jesus*; Robbins, *Jesus the Teacher*; W. H. Kelber, "Apostolic Tradition and the Form of the Gospel," in *Discipleship in the New Testament*, ed. F. F. Segovia (Philadelphia: Fortress Press, 1985), 24-46. For a survey of recent scholarly research on discipleship in Mark's Gospel, see Matera, *What Are They Saying About Mark?* chap. 3.

2. See, e.g., M. Hengel, *The Charismatic Leader and His Followers* (SNTW; New York: Crossroad, 1981), 50-57.

3. Apart from 1:18 and 1:20, clear examples of passages in which to "follow" Jesus or to "come after" him connotes accompanying Jesus as his disciple are 2:14; 8:34; 10:21 (in which case the man refuses Jesus' summons to accompany him as his disciple); 10:28; and 15:41. By contrast, compare with these a passage such as 14:13, where to "follow" is simply used literally to mean "going after a person in time and place" and cannot be understood to connote accompaniment as a disciple. Further passages in which "following" Jesus is apparently also being used in its literal sense are 3:7; 5:24; 10:52 (contrary to scholarly opinion, Jesus does not make Bartimaeus a disciple, for the command Jesus gives him to "go" is a term of dismissal and not a term signifying the call to discipleship; Bartimaeus "goes" by joining the crowd trailing Jesus on his way up to Jerusalem [see 10:46]; Kingsbury, *Christology of Mark's Gospel*, 104 n. 159); 11:9; 14:54. Passages in which it is not immediately apparent whether "following" Jesus does or does not connote accompaniment as his disciple are 2:15; 6:1; 9:38; (10:32; are those following Jesus the crowd, as at 10:46?).

4. This statement is not mitigated by the pericope on Jesus' true family (3:31-35). To be sure, in this pericope the crowd is in fact contrasted with Jesus' natural family (his mother and his brothers): Whereas the crowd is sitting "about Jesus," his natural family is described as standing "outside." The words Jesus speaks to the crowd, however, do not declare the crowd to be disciples or "true family" but instead constitute a challenge: "See, my mother and my brothers; whoever does the will of God is my brother, and sister, and mother" (3:34-35). That these words of Jesus are not to be interpreted as characterizing the crowd per se as his disciples can be seen already in 4:1-12. Here Jesus teaches the crowd in parables (4:1-2), narrating the parable of the sower (4:3-9). As soon as he finishes this parable, Mark writes at 4:10-12 that "those 'about him' with the twelve" ask Jesus concerning the parable(s). The thing to note is that these persons "about Jesus" who are with the twelve are said by Mark to be "alone," that is to say, separated from the crowd. It is to these "about Jesus" and the twelve that Jesus declares, "To you is given the secret of the kingdom of God; but for those outside everything is in parables" (4:11). In other words, it is to disciples of Jesus that the secret is given (see also 4:34), and Mark has drawn a dividing line between disciples and crowd. In brief,

then, Mark can be seen to distinguish sharply in 3:31-35; 4:1-12 among (*a*) the natural family of Jesus, (*b*) the crowd, and (*c*) Jesus' disciples. In any event, the statement holds: Although the crowd is favorably disposed toward Jesus (3:31-35) and Jesus summons the crowd to discipleship (8:34), Mark does not portray the crowd as such as a huge throng of disciples.

5. Cf., e.g., Mark 6:7 with 6:30-31 and 6:35; 9:31 with 9:33-35; 11:11 with 11:12-14; 14:17 with 14:32.

6. On the women at the crucifixion as being disciples of Jesus, see Dewey, *Disciples of the Way*, 131-34.

7. See, e.g., Mark 8:29, 32-33; 9:5-6; 10:28; 11:14 with 11:21-22; 14:29-31. Also Brown-Donfried-Reumann, *Peter in the New Testament*, 61.

8. See, e.g., Mark 1:36-37; 8:29; 9:5-6; 14:29-31, 37-38. Also Brown-Donfried-Reumann, *Peter in the New Testament*, 61-62.

9. For a good discussion of the textual evidence concerning James and Levi, see Best, *Following Jesus*, 176-77.

10. See J. Donahue, "Tax Collectors and Sinners," *CBQ* 33 (1971): 54, 59.

11. On the importance of the "mountain" as a setting in Mark, see Malbon, *Narrative Space and Mythic Meaning*, 84-89.

12. Ibid., 84.

13. At points throughout his story, Mark echoes the notion that disciples of Jesus are "with him" (see, e.g., 3:7; [5:18]; 5:37, 40; 8:10; 11:11; 14:14, 17, 33, 67).

14. Scholarly opinion on the interpretation of Jesus' parable discourse in Mark 4 or parts thereof diverges widely. For a sampling of various views, see, e.g., J. R. Donahue, *The Gospel in Parable: Metaphor, Narrative, and Theology in the Synoptic Gospels* (Philadelphia: Fortress Press, 1988), 28-52; C. E. Carlston, *The Parables of the Triple Tradition* (Philadelphia: Fortress Press, 1975), 97-210; W. H. Kelber, *The Kingdom in Mark: A New Place and a New Time* (Philadelphia: Fortress Press, 1974), 25-43; Boucher, *Mysterious Parable*, 42-63, 80-84; and Marcus, *Mystery of the Kingdom of God*.

15. The "secret," or "mystery," of the kingdom of God given the disciples is understood by scholars in vastly different ways. The following views are representative of this diversity: Achtemeier (*Mark*, 73) understands the mystery the disciples receive as "fellowship with Jesus." Kelber (*Kingdom in Mark*, 37-41) regards it as pointing to the hiddenness of the kingdom in Jesus and in the present of Mark's own day and to its future appearance in glory.

S. Brown ("The Secret of the Kingdom of God [Mark 4:11]," *JBL* 92 [1973]: 74) argues that the secret refers to "secret instruction" given the twelve which, in post-Easter times, they will pass on to the Christian community. Petersen (*Literary Criticism*, 68) holds that the secret is to be defined in terms of "Jesus' identity as the Son of man who must die, rise, and return." Donahue (*Gospel in Parable*, 44-46) avers that the mystery of the kingdom is that "the reign or power of God is now manifest in the brokenness of Jesus on the cross, his hiddenness which is to be revealed." Via (*Ethics of Mark's Gospel*, 188-90) contends that the mystery of the kingdom and the mystery of Jesus' suffering, death, and resurrection are one and the same and that, paradoxically, this mystery is both inexhaustible and yet qualified by the narrative Mark tells. Williams (*Gospel against Parable*, 44) defines the mystery in similar fashion as the sacrificial suffering of the Son of man. J. Marcus ("Mark 4:10-12 and Marcan Epistemology," *JBL* 103 [1984]: 563-67) asserts that the mystery of the kingdom "has to do with God's strange design of bringing his kingdom in Jesus Christ, yet unleashing the forces of darkness to blind human beings so that they oppose that kingdom." Finally, Rhoads and Michie (*Mark as Story*, 90-91) opine that what the secret is is simply never stated in any straightforward way.

In determining the meaning of the "secret" of the kingdom, one does well not to lose sight of the following observation: Because it is in response to a question concerning "parables" that Jesus says that the secret of God's kingdom "has been given and presently belongs to" (perfect tense) the disciples, one is invited to look to the parables of Mark 4 to ascertain the meaning of the secret of the kingdom, which is what we have done in the body of our study.

16. See Mark 4:3-9, 26-29, 30-32; also 10:13-16.
17. See Mark 1:14-15; 4:3, 14.
18. See Mark 3:14-15.
19. Cf. Mark 6:12 with 1:14-15.
20. Cf. Mark 6:30 with 1:21-22; 6:6b.
21. Cf. Mark 6:13 with 1:34; 3:10.
22. Cf. Mark 6:13 with 1:34, 39.
23. See Taylor, *St. Mark*, 306; and Gnilka, *Evangelium nach Markus*, 240-41.
24. See Mark 1:21-22, 23-28, 32-34, 38-39; 2:8-12; 3:10-12.
25. See Mark 4:14-20.
26. On the significance of the "boat" in Mark, see Malbon, *Narrative Space and Mythic Meaning*, 100-101.

27. The translation of this latter question is that of the New Jerusalem Bible.

28. For a discussion of this motif, see J. P. Heil, *Jesus Walking on the Sea: Meaning and Gospel Functions of Matt 14:22-33, Mark 6:45-52 and John 6:15b-21* (AnBib 87; Rome: Biblical Institute Press, 1981), 69-72.

29. See, e.g., Mark 9:28-29, 38-50; 10:10-12, 23-31, 42-45; 12:43-44; chap. 13.

30. See esp. 10:2-12; 11:12—12:34.

31. The difficulty with this passage, of course, is that it presents the Markan Jesus as predicting the consummation of the age in less than a generation's time. For a brief overview of scholarly attempts to explain this passage, see Cranfield, *St Mark*, 285-89; Nineham, *St Mark*, 231-32; and Pesch, *Markusevangelium*, 2:66-67.

32. On the inferior social status of children in first-century Jewish society, see J. Jeremias, *Jerusalem in the Time of Jesus: An Investigation Into Economic and Social Conditions During the New Testament Period* (Philadelphia: Fortress Press, 1969), 375.

33. Situated in the Jordan Valley, Jericho lies approximately fifteen miles northeast of Jerusalem.

34. So Cranfield, *St Mark*, 415-16.

35. Perhaps the most eloquent spokesperson for this position is Kelber (*Mark's Story of Jesus*, 75-77, 84-85; and "Apostolic Tradition and the Form of the Gospel," 37-40).

36. For a strong presentation of this position, see N. Petersen, "When Is the End Not the End?" *Int* 34 (1980): 151-66.

37. See Kingsbury, *Christology of Mark's Gospel*, 133-37.

Selected
Bibliography

Achtemeier, Paul J. *Mark*. 2d ed., rev. and enl. PC. Philadelphia: Fortress Press, 1986.

This book, first published in 1975, has served as the standard introduction to Mark for more than a decade. While Achtemeier's approach is that of redaction criticism, he also surveys literary-critical studies in chapter 5 on Mark as literature.

Best, Ernest. *Following Jesus: Discipleship in the Gospel of Mark*. JSNTSup 4. Sheffield: JSOT Press, 1981.

In this redaction-critical study, Best explores the theme of discipleship under three main headings: the disciple and the cross; the disciple and the world; and the disciple in the community.

_____. *Mark: The Gospel as Story*. Edinburgh: T. & T. Clark, 1983.

Despite the reference to "story" in the subtitle, this work is redaction-critical in character. Best views Mark's Gospel as a compilation of traditions and ably discusses on this basis its unity, nature, purpose, audience, and theology.

Boring, M. Eugene. *Truly Human/Truly Divine: Christological Language and the Gospel Form*. St. Louis: CBP Press, 1984.

Writing with the non-specialist in mind, Boring shows how the gospel, as a literary form, incorporates within it a double image of Jesus: On the one hand, Jesus is (like us) weak, the crucified man from Nazareth; on the other hand, he is (not like us) strong, the powerful Son of God.

Dewey, Joanna. *Markan Public Debate: Literary Technique, Concentric Structure, and Theology in Mark 2:1—3:6.* SBLDS 48. Chico, Calif.: Scholars Press, 1980.
  In this rhetorical-critical study, Dewey examines the overall structure of Mark 2:1—3:6 and the literary techniques according to which it was composed so as to understand both the interrelationships among the various parts of the section and its meaning as a whole.

Donahue, John R. *Are You the Christ? The Trial Narrative in the Gospel of Mark.* SBLDS 10. Missoula, Mont.: Society of Biblical Literature, 1973.
  Although his focus is on Mark's account of the trial of Jesus (14:53-65), Donahue treats a broad range of other topics as well, including the anti-temple theme and such key christological terms as "Christ," "Son of God," and "the Son of man."

Fowler, Robert M. *Loaves and Fishes: The Function of the Feeding Stories in the Gospel of Mark.* SBLDS 54. Chico, Calif.: Scholars Press, 1981.
  The major thesis of this literary-critical investigation is that the story of the feeding of the five thousand is a Markan composition. A chapter on reader-response criticism and on the implied reader of Mark round it out.

Hengel, Martin. *Studies in the Gospel of Mark.* Philadelphia: Fortress Press, 1985.
  In these three studies, Hengel concentrates mainly on the historical origins of Mark's Gospel. He argues for a reappropriation of the traditional views that the Gospel was written in Rome in A.D. 69 and contains materials handed down by Peter through John Mark (referred to in Acts 12).

Juel, Donald. *Messiah and Temple: The Trial of Jesus in the Gospel of Mark.* SBLDS 31. Missoula, Mont.: Scholars Press, 1977.
  As the subtitle indicates, the focus of this study is on the trial of Jesus. Juel approaches Mark's account of the trial at the literary level and explains the role it plays both within the passion narrative and the Gospel as a whole.

Kee, Howard Clark. *Community of the New Age: Studies in Mark's Gospel.* Philadelphia: Westminster Press, 1977.

After locating the origins of Mark's Gospel in rural and small-town Syria, Kee argues that it was written in the late 60s and patterned after Jewish apocalyptic writings.

Kelber, Werner H. *Mark's Story of Jesus.* Philadelphia: Fortress Press, 1979.

This book is an interpretive retelling of Mark's story of the life and death of Jesus, understood as a journey beginning in Galilee and ending in Jerusalem. Noteworthy is Kelber's espousal of the view, long debated by scholars, that Mark depicts the disciples at the close of his story as permanently alienated from Jesus.

————, ed. *The Passion in Mark: Studies on Mark 14–16.* Philadelphia: Fortress Press, 1976.

In these redaction-critical studies written by a team of scholars, each pericope in Mark's passion account is investigated in terms both of the role it plays within the passion account itself and of the thematic links it exhibits to other parts of the Gospel.

Kingsbury, Jack Dean. *The Christology of Mark's Gospel.* Philadelphia: Fortress Press, 1983.

This investigation uses literary method to reappraise Mark's portrait of Jesus. Following brief chapters on the "messianic secret" and recent approaches to Mark's understanding of Jesus, it shows how Mark, in the course of his story, gradually unveils the identity of Jesus. In chapter 5, it deals with the special way in which "the Son of man" is used.

Malbon, Elizabeth Struthers. *Narrative Space and Mythic Meaning in Mark.* NVBS. San Francisco: Harper & Row, 1986.

The purpose of this book is to illuminate Mark's gospel story by investigating the spatial references found in it: heaven vs. earth, land vs. sea, Jewish homeland vs. foreign land, Galilee vs. Judea, isolated areas vs. inhabited areas, house vs. synagogue, Mount of Olives vs. temple, and tomb vs. mountain.

Marcus, Joel. *The Mystery of the Kingdom of God.* SBLDS 90. Atlanta: Scholars Press, 1986.

The thesis of this redaction-critical analysis of Mark's parable chapter is that whereas the stress in 4:3-20 is on the hiddenness of the kingdom, in 4:21-32 it is on the kingdom's moving from hiddenness to manifestation.

Martin, Ralph P. *Mark: Evangelist and Theologian*. CEP. Grand Rapids: Zondervan, 1973.
This study deals with the origins of Mark's Gospel so as to understand the Gospel in the light of them. Martin's contention is that by telling of Jesus' suffering Messiahship, Mark gives encouragement to his own persecuted church in Rome and summons it to faithful discipleship.

Marxsen, Willi. *Mark the Evangelist: Studies on the Redaction History of the Gospel*. Translated by Roy A. Harrisville et al. Nashville: Abingdon Press, 1969.
This monograph, first published in German in 1956, is generally credited with inaugurating the redaction-critical approach to Mark's Gospel. Marxsen's discussion of this approach in the introduction is classic.

Matera, Frank J. *The Kingship of Jesus: Composition and Theology in Mark 15*. SBLDS 66. Chico, Calif.: Scholars Press, 1982.
As the subtitle suggests, this study shows how Mark has composed chapter 15 of his passion account in such fashion as to highlight a royal theology that comes to climactic expression in the centurion's confession of Jesus as the Son of God.

————. *What Are They Saying About Mark?* New York: Paulist Press, 1987.
This survey of the last twenty-five years of Markan research discusses, in a nontechnical way, scholarly views on five major topics: the setting in which Mark's Gospel arose; Mark's understanding of Jesus and of discipleship; principles Mark used in composing his Gospel; and present-day literary approaches to Mark's Gospel.

Perrin, Norman. *A Modern Pilgrimage in New Testament Christology*. Philadelphia: Fortress Press, 1974.
In these essays, Perrin focuses on the Christology of Mark and especially on Mark's use of "the Son of man."

Petersen, Norman R. *Literary Criticism for New Testament Critics*. GBS. Philadelphia: Fortress Press, 1978.
In chapter 3, Petersen investigates the whole of Mark's narrative. He wants to show that Mark locates the resolution of the plot of his story in the meeting that the young man in white (following Jesus' own words) predicts Jesus will have with the disciples in Galilee. The reader is invited to project that at this meeting the disciples finally shed the ignorance besetting them.

Rhoads, David, and Donald Michie. *Mark as Story: An Introduction to the Narrative of a Gospel.* Philadelphia: Fortress Press, 1982.
History will show that more than any other single work, this book has pointed the way to a literary (narrative-critical) study of Mark's Gospel. Following an English translation of the Greek, the authors treat, in turn, the rhetoric, settings, plot, and characters of the story of Mark.

Robbins, Vernon K. *Jesus the Teacher: A Socio-Rhetorical Interpretation of Mark.* Philadelphia: Fortress Press, 1984.
This book is a study in socio-rhetorical criticism. Robbins understands Mark to have combined in his Gospel biblical-Jewish and Greco-Roman traditions and conventions. Mark's Jesus is at once biblical prophet and Greco-Roman philosopher and teacher; he fulfills Jewish messianic expectations in a way that would capture the attention of non-Jews of Mediterranean society.

Senior, Donald. *The Passion of Jesus in the Gospel of Mark.* Wilmington, Del.: Michael Glazier, 1984.
In this book, Senior provides a detailed, yet eminently readable, analysis of the passion account of Mark. He introduces this analysis by surveying the material leading up to the passion account and he follows it with a discussion of the theology of the account.

Via, Dan O., Jr. *The Ethics of Mark's Gospel in the Middle of Time.* Philadelphia: Fortress Press, 1985.
Via here explores the ethical teachings of Mark's Gospel and especially of chapter 10 within the context of the Markan narrative itself. His larger concern is to explore the implications the Markan narrative holds for faith and conduct in today's world.

Williams, James G. *Gospel Against Parable: Mark's Language of Mystery.* BLS 12. Sheffield: Almond, 1985.
The contention of Williams's book is that Mark is a narrative-gospel, the product of bringing together "biography" and "parable." Mark sets forth the mystery of the kingdom as revealed in "the way" of Jesus, the suffering Son of man.

Index

145

148 *Index*